A BRIDGE TO OUR TRADITION: PIRKEI AVOT

by
Nachama Skolnik Moskowitz

Illustrated by
Joseph Cooper

Project Editor
Faye Tillis Lewy

D1299563

**Dedicated to
Zac, Shira, and Jacob,
and all those who will
cross the Bridge with them.**

Overview to פִּרְקֵי אָבוֹת (Pirkei Avot)

Jews have long been known as the People of the Book. The central or most "famous" Jewish book is the תּוֹרָה (Torah), which is filled with the stories, laws, and ethical standards that guide our actions and beliefs. According to Jewish tradition, at Mount Sinai God passed along to Moses both a specific, written Torah and an oral version.

- The **written** Torah is known as the Five Books of Moses and contains Genesis (*B'reishit*—בְּרֵאשִׁית), Exodus (*Sh'mot*—שְׁמוֹת), Leviticus (*Vayikra*—וַיִּקְרָא), Numbers (*B'midbar*—בְּמִדְבַּר), and Deuteronomy (*D'varim*—דְּבָרִים).

- The **oral** Torah comprises those laws and ideas that the Jewish people passed along verbally from generation to generation. Almost 1500 years after Mount Sinai, a rabbi named Judah HaNasi (Judah the Prince) is said to have organized what had been taught by word of mouth and written it down into a book we now call the Mishnah (מִשְׁנָה). Pirkei Avot (אָבוֹת פִּרְקֵי), the book that forms the foundation of this worktext, is part of the מִשְׁנָה.*

Quick Facts

1. The Hebrew word פֶּרֶק (*perek*) means chapter.
2. There are six chapters, or פְּרָקִים (*p'rakim*), in פִּרְקֵי אָבוֹת (Chapters of the Fathers).
3. "The fathers" refers to the men quoted in the book, all well-known rabbis who lived around 1,800–2,200 years ago.
4. Each chapter is divided into smaller sections, called מִשְׁנָה (*mishnah*). The plural is מִשְׁנָיוֹת (*mishnayot*).
5. פִּרְקֵי אָבוֹת is found in most prayer books and is studied by Jews between Pesach and Shavuot, as well as at other times.

6. The words and ideas of פִּרְקֵי אָבוֹת are so popular that their words are found in many youth group and synagogue songs today. Some examples are

אִם אֵין אֲנִי לִי מִי לִי (*Im ein ani li, mi li*)

לֹא עָלֶיךָ הַמְּלָאכָה לִגְמוֹר (*Lo alecha hamlachah ligmor*)

בְּמָקוֹם שֶׁאֵין אֲנָשִׁים (*B'makom she-ein anashim*)

עַל שְׁלֹשָׁה דְבָרִים (*Al sh'loshah d'varim*)

* For further details on the background of Pirkei Avot, see the Forward and Introduction to *Pirke Avot: A Modern Commentary on Jewish Ethics*, by Leonard Kravitz and Kerry M. Olitzky (NY: UAHC Press, 1993).

Introduction to This Book

Most books about פִּרְקֵי אָבוֹת begin with chapter one and end with chapter six. However, in creating this book I decided to look for themes among the various sayings. I cut up all the מִשְׁנָיוֹת, sorted them, and then chose the three "Big Questions" I felt were most compelling for young adolescents:

- What are the character traits that help define who we are as individuals?
- What are the ways we can interact positively with others?
- What are our responsibilities to improve the world?

Even after cutting up and rearranging the text, however, I felt it important for students to see פִּרְקֵי אָבוֹת in its entirety, the way it was organized by Judah HaNasi. Therefore, a full version of פִּרְקֵי אָבוֹת is provided at the end of this book; after all, we are a People of the Book, not of the Workbook.

My own daughter taught me about the dangers of "adult blah-blah," by her definition the times when a teacher does a lot of talking, or a textbook is filled with words upon words of explanation. In writing this book, I tried hard not to "blah-blah," but rather to invite students to discover our Jewish tradition as full participants in an interactive community of learners. Rather than tell students what the rabbis had to say about ethical living, I offer opportunities for them to explore the rabbis' thoughts either alone or in small, cooperative groups.

Each chapter is similarly structured:

Text from פִּרְקֵי אָבוֹת

The English follows the translation of Leonard Kravitz and Kerry M. Olitzky's book, *Pirke Avot: A Modern Commentary on Jewish Ethics* (NY: UAHC Press, 1993), with some exceptions. In a few circumstances, when the English was a bit complex, I altered the translation. These shifts are noted in the Teacher's Guide.

The English and Hebrew are set up to mirror each other; students with some Hebrew background may either use the English to help them access the translation or cover up the English and study just the Hebrew.

A Beginning Thought

All activities for each chapter either build out of, or lead back to, the Beginning Thought. In reality, this is the Big Idea that serves as the foundation of the chapter.

Activities

Each activity helps students better understand the text from פִּרְקֵי אָבוֹת. Most contain questions to be explored with one or more students in small, cooperative groupings. At times, students work with graphic organizers (charts, diagrams) or other texts that offer additional insights into the Big Idea.

An Ending Thought from You

Each chapter ends with an opportunity for students to apply the Big Idea to their own lives; this section is usually completed individually.

It is recommended that teachers refer to the accompanying Teacher's Guide for ideas, resources, and teaching suggestions.

Acknowledgments

A Bridge to Our Tradition: Pirkei Avot does not follow the normative textbook format familiar to most teachers. I am most appreciative to Rabbi Hara Person and others at UAHC Press for taking a leap of faith to bring this worktext to light. They provided me with a most wonderful editor, Faye Tillis Lewy, who read each word carefully, helped reshape areas of text that were confusing, and worked with me to track down elusive supplementary ideas and materials. I thank her for her incredible help.

Joseph Cooper did a wonderful job with the illustrations and Itzhack Shelomi masterfully created the book design. Ken Gesser, Stuart Benick, Liane Broido, Rick Abrams, and Rachel Gleiberman all played important roles in bringing this book to life. My thanks to them all.

For teachers, successful use of *A Bridge to Our Tradition: Pirkei Avot* means changing the traditional model of the teacher as provider-of-information-to-students to that of one-who-facilitates-learning. It means helping students learn to ask their own questions and guiding them in finding answers. For students, success means taking an active role as learner, wrestling with texts and ideas in ways normally not part of Jewish education at this age. I appreciate those willing to work "outside the box"; the results are well worth it.

Finally, I thank my own children, who not only provided for me an image of the learner for whom this book was written, but allowed me precious time to complete the manuscript.

Nachama Skolnik Moskowitz
Cleveland, Ohio

5761

Logistical Notes

Use of Texts

For decades, many of the textbooks used by students in Jewish schools offered summaries of the great texts of our tradition; students were given a modern author's retelling of a great textual document (for example, the Torah). In this worktext, students are given direct translations of most texts, whether Bible narratives or selections from the Talmud or midrash. The language has been simplified in some instances to make the text accessible to students working with each other in small groups with teacher guidance.

Symbols

  Individual work

  Paired work

  Small group work

Hebrew Glossary

Not only is each text given in Hebrew and English, but basic Hebrew words appear throughout the book, promoting the message that Hebrew is integral to Jewish study. To assist teachers and students who cannot read Hebrew, a definition and transliteration is offered on or near the page where a word first appears and again at the end of the book. All Hebrew and English words so defined appear in boldface the first time they are mentioned in the text.

English Glossary

When difficult English words are used that students may not know, a definition is offered on or near the page and again at the end of the book.

Contents

Unit 1

IF I AM NOT FOR MYSELF, WHO WILL BE FOR ME?

THE CROWN OF A GOOD NAME

Rabbi Shimon said,
"There are three crowns:

רַבִּי שִׁמְעוֹן אוֹמֵר
שְׁלשָׁה כְתָרִים הֵן:

the crown of Torah;

כֶּתֶר תּוֹרָה

---

priesthood

In the Torah, God commands Aaron and his family to serve as the כֹּהֲנִים *(kohanim)*, or priests, taking care of the rituals in the desert Tabernacle, and later at the Temple in Jerusalem. This service is called the priesthood.

---

the crown of **priesthood**;

וְכֶתֶר כְּהֻנָּה

and the crown of royalty.

וְכֶתֶר מַלְכוּת.

However, the crown of a good name is greater than all of them."

וְכֶתֶר שֵׁם טוֹב
עוֹלָה עַל גַּבֵּיהֶן.

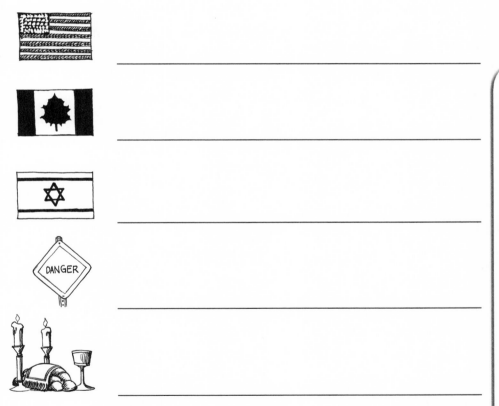

A Beginning Thought: An object may help us understand an idea.

Our brains are remarkable! As the center of our nervous system, the brain helps our hands to move, our eyes to see, and our tongues to taste. Our brain also gives us the ability to look at an object and understand a bigger idea.

 Take a look at the objects below, and make a note explaining what each one symbolizes.

_____

_____

_____

_____

_____

מִשְׁנָה

A small piece of text, like a verse from the Bible, but found in the Jewish books known as the Mishnah and the Talmud, which were written more than 1,500 years ago. In this worktext, the word מִשְׁנָה (mishnah) will appear in Hebrew when referring to the small piece of text. When referring to the book, the English "Mishnah" will be used.

Our מִשְׁנָה begins with Rabbi Shimon telling us about crowns. However, Rabbi Shimon has a bigger idea to teach us about people by the time this מִשְׁנָה is done!

The Big Ideas of Each Crown

 Find a partner. Together, spend a couple of minutes looking over the chart. Then, in the empty column, write down some of the "Big Ideas" the two of you think each crown might symbolize.

The crown	"Who" wears it?	What else might be interesting to know?	What Big Ideas might the crown symbolize?
	The Torah scroll "wears" a crown when it is sitting in the אֲרוֹן הַקֹדֶשׁ or when it is carried around the synagogue before it is read.	The Torah is dressed as it is to remind us of the clothing הַכֹּהֵן הַגָּדוֹל wore when leading worship services.	
	The Torah tells us that Aaron (Moses' brother) wore a special crown when he served as הַכֹּהֵן הַגָּדוֹל, leading the Israelites in worship in the desert.	For more than a thousand years after Aaron, each הַכֹּהֵן הַגָּדוֹל wore the crown while leading the worship service, both in the desert and at the Temple in Jerusalem.	
	A king or queen wears a crown when involved in formal ceremonial events.	There are many different styles of royal crowns: big, small, plain, fancy.	

As a class, share some of your thoughts about these crowns and the bigger ideas each crown symbolizes.

_____

_____

 Rabbi Shimon says that a **כֶּתֶר שֵׁם טוֹב**, a **crown of a good name**, is better than any of these three crowns. But what does it mean to have a good name? Whom do we know who has a **שֵׁם טוֹב**? Spend some time exploring this question in small groups by finding out more about some Jews in the Bible with a **שֵׁם טוֹב**.

שֵׁם טוֹב

Who in the Bible Has a שֵׁם טוֹב?

 Divide into small groups to research one or two of the biblical characters listed on the following pages. Your goal is to figure out the qualities of someone with a **שֵׁם טוֹב**. To help your group work together well, consider sharing these jobs:

READER: This person reads the verses aloud, while other group members read along.

LEADER: This person leads the discussion as your group looks for clues to the qualities of someone with a **שֵׁם טוֹב**.

REPORTER: This person reports back to the class some of your group's findings.

כֶּתֶר שֵׁם טוֹב

"Crown of a good name."

crown = כֶּתֶר
(keter)

name = שֵׁם
(shem)

good = טוֹב (tov)

שֵׁם טוֹב

Good name
(shem tov).

Biblical person	Verses from the Bible	What is the story about?	What did the person do that was good?
Avraham (Abraham)	Genesis 18:1–8		
Avraham (Abraham)	Genesis 18:20–33		
Rivkah (Rebecca)	Genesis 24:1–20		
Moshe (Moses)	Exodus 18:13–16		

Biblical Person	Verses from the Bible	What is the story about?	What did the person do that was good?
Moshe (Moses)	Exodus 32:1–14		
Rachav (Rahab)	Joshua 2:1–16		
Shlomo (King Solomon)	I Kings 3:5–14		
Shlomo (King Solomon)	I Kings 3:16–28		

Discuss your group's answers. Then, using the stories and actions of the biblical people as a guide, make a list inside the crown below of the characteristics of a person who has earned a שֵׁם טוֹב.

_____

_____

_____

_____

_____

An Ending Thought from You

- Rabbi Shimon uses crowns to help us understand a bigger idea about

_____

_____

_____

- I would give a כֶּתֶר שֵׁם טוֹב to the following three people alive today:

1) _____ because _____.

2) _____ because _____.

3) _____ because _____.

BEN ZOMA ASKS, "WHO?"

Ben Zoma said,
"Who is wise?

בֶּן זוֹמָא אוֹמֵר
אֵיזֶהוּ חָכָם?

The one who learns from
everyone, as it says,
'From all who would teach me,
have I gained understanding....'

[PSALM 119:99]

הַלוֹמֵד מִכָּל אָדָם
שֶׁנֶּאֱמַר
מִכָּל מְלַמְּדַי הִשְׂכַּלְתִּי...

Who is mighty?

אֵיזֶהוּ גִבּוֹר?

One who controls one's
[natural] urges, as it says,
'One who is slow to anger is
better than the mighty and one
who rules one's spirit than one who
conquers a city.'

[PROVERBS 16:32]

הַכּוֹבֵשׁ אֶת יִצְרוֹ
שֶׁנֶּאֱמַר
טוֹב אֶרֶךְ אַפַּיִם מִגִּבּוֹר
וּמוֹשֵׁל בְּרוּחוֹ מִלֹּכֵד
עִיר.

Who is rich? אֵיזֶהוּ עָשִׁיר?

One who is happy
with what one
has, as it says,
'When you eat
what your hands
have provided, you shall be happy
and good will be yours....'

הַשָּׂמֵחַ בְּחֶלְקוֹ
שֶׁנֶּאֱמַר יְגִיעַ כַּפֶּיךָ
כִּי תֹאכֵל אַשְׁרֶיךָ
וְטוֹב לָךְ....

[PSALM 128:2]

despise

To think of
something as
worthless; to
scorn.

———

**lightly
esteemed**

Not valued;
held in low
regard.

Who is honored? אֵיזֶהוּ מְכֻבָּד?

One who honors others,
as it says, 'Those who
honor Me, I will honor,
and those who **despise** Me,
will be **lightly esteemed**.'"

הַמְכַבֵּד אֶת הַבְּרִיּוֹת
שֶׁנֶּאֱמַר כִּי מְכַבְּדַי
אֲכַבֵּד וּבֹזַי יֵקָלּוּ.

[I SAMUEL 2:30]

A Beginning Thought: When a person acts with respect to others, he or she earns respect in return.

In the last lesson, you considered Rabbi Shimon's opinion that it is important to earn "the crown of a שֵׁם טוֹב." Take a moment and think about the reason others might crown you with a שֵׁם טוֹב.

Circle your own good qualities. Feel free to add other qualities not already listed.

smart	helpful	friendly	serious	strong
kind	happy	considerate	truthful	rich
thoughtful	pleasant	patient	generous	supportive
good listener	sympathetic	creative	wise	_____
_____	_____	_____	_____	_____

What Makes Someone a Good Friend?

 Pair up with another student and choose four qualities from your list above that would make someone a good friend. Be ready to discuss your choices with your classmates.

Characteristics we chose	Reasons
1._____	1._____
2._____	2._____
3._____	3._____
4._____	4._____

 Share your lists with one another. In a small group, decide what the top six qualities of a good friend are. Do you agree with these six choices?

Looking at Ben Zoma's Words

In this מִשְׁנָה, a rabbi named Ben Zoma asks *how* we know if someone has certain personal characteristics. He chooses to talk about those who are:

Wise　　　　**Mighty**　　　　**Rich**　　　　**Honorable**

Ben Zoma describes four personal qualities, but he does *not* say that a person has to have all four qualities. So, for example:

> A person could be wise.
>
> A person could be mighty.
>
> A person could be rich and mighty.
>
> A person could be honorable.
>
> A person could be wise, rich, and honorable.

A person could be any combination of these four!

Ben Zoma also writes in a pattern that helps us understand his thinking.

- First, he asks a question.
- Next, he gives an answer.
- Next, he shares a quote from the Bible that explains why his answer is a good one.

 Form a group of three. Choose one member to read the questions, one to read the answers, and the third to read the quotes. Next, turn to Ben Zoma's מִשְׁנָה on pages (9–10) and take turns reading each of the questions, answers, and quotes. Do you see Ben Zoma's pattern?

What Does Ben Zoma Mean?

 Ben Zoma tells us something about people that might surprise us! Use his quote to help you fill in the blanks below.

1. According to Ben Zoma, a wise person might not necessarly get straight A's.

   He says that a wise person _____

   _____.

   Whom do you know who is wise as defined by Ben Zoma? _____

2. According to Ben Zoma, a rich person does not have to have a lot of money.

   He says that a rich person _____

   _____.

   Whom do you know who is rich as defined by Ben Zoma? _____

3. According to Ben Zoma, a mighty person might not be physically strong. He

   says that a mighty person _____

   _____.

   Whom do you know who is mighty as defined by Ben Zoma?_____

4. According to Ben Zoma, a person we honor might not receive an award. He

   says that an honored person _____

   _____.

   Whom do you know who is honored as defined by Ben Zoma?_____

Smile, Thinking about Ben Zoma

If Ben Zoma lived in our time, he might have enjoyed finding a cartoon that illustrated his answers. Read the cartoons below and write Ben Zoma's matching question under each. Be careful—the cartoons are not in order of Ben Zoma's words!

I'M GOING TO PUT THIS ON THE HALLWAY OF FAME.

Who is _____?   ?_____ אֵיזֶהוּ

I HAD TO DO SOMETHING. JEFFREY WAS MAKING FUN OF EVERYONE!

I'M PROUD THAT YOU STOOD UP TO HIM, EMILY. BUT, I'M CONCERNED THAT YOU MAY BE IN DANGER.

LET THE PRINCIPAL AND TEACHERS TAKE CARE OF THINGS FROM NOW ON.

Who is _____?   ?_____ אֵיזֶהוּ

Who is _____? ? _____אֵיזֶהוּ

Who is _____? ? _____אֵיזֶהוּ

An Ending Thought from You

Ben Zoma tells us that a wise person might not know more than anyone else, that someone rich does not have to have a lot of money, that a mighty person might not be physically strong, and that a person we honor might not be an award winner! Rather, Ben Zoma teaches us that these good characteristics really are about the way a person respects other people—and gets respect in return.

- In what ways do *you* earn the respect of others?

_____

_____

_____

- What would Ben Zoma say about you?

Who is_____? One who _____.

PURSUING HONOR

In **פִּרְקֵי אָבוֹת** 4:1 Ben Zoma says that a person who is honored is one who honors others. Other rabbis, however, offer different thoughts about honor. In this chapter, we will briefly look at two other *mishnayot* from פִּרְקֵי אָבוֹת that discuss honor. The first מִשְׁנָה is on this page. The second is on page 21.

4:21

Rabbi Elazar HaKappar said,	רַבִּי אֶלְעָזָר הַקַּפָּר אוֹמֵר
"**Envy**,	הַקִּנְאָה
desire,	וְהַתַּאֲוָה
and [the pursuit of] honor	וְהַכָּבוֹד
take a person out of this world."	מוֹצִיאִין אֶת הָאָדָם מִן הָעוֹלָם.

envy
To resent someone else's achievements or possessions.

———

desire
To want or wish for something.

A Beginning Thought: Who is rich? One who is happy with what one has!

YOU MEAN TO TELL ME NO ONE WANTED TO BE A CONTESTANT?

In 1999, a TV game show called *Who Wants to Be a Millionaire?* became instantly popular. On the show, contestants used their knowledge to try and win $1,000,000. From that beginning, other "games" came to TV, including *Survivor* (sixteen people moved to a primitive island to compete for a prize of $1,000,000). The participitants wanted fame and fortune. Many who watched these shows envied the contestants, especially the winners. But there were others who wondered about the values these shows promoted. They asked whether it was possible to be a good person ("pursue honor") when greed was so important.

The author of the cartoon above thought about this question. "Mensch" is a Yiddish word meaning "quality person." A mensch is kind, considerate, and helpful. He or she is the type of person you'd want for a friend. Look at the cartoon and think about the values of a show that focuses on being a mensch.

 With a partner, brainstorm about the kind of game that contestants would play on *Who Wants to Be a Mensch*?

What Does Elazar HaKappar Want to Tell Us?

Elazar HaKappar would say that a mensch does not "envy" others, "desire" other people's things, or focus on the "pursuit of honor." But what does that really mean for us today?

 With a partner, do the following things in this order:

1. Write "E" on any kids who are showing that they envy someone.
2. Write "D" on any kids who are showing that they desire something.
3. Write "PH" on any kids who are showing that they want to pursue honor.

Two Sides of the Same Coin

In English there is a saying, "Such-and-such is like two sides of the same coin." This means that two thoughts or ideas are related—they are on the same coin—but that they each mean something different—they are on different sides of the coin.

Ben Zoma and Rabbi Elazar HaKappar each expressed thoughts that might be considered "two sides of the same coin." Your job is to figure out how that could be.

With your partner, complete the chart below.

Think about Elazar HaKappar's side of the coin:	Think about Ben Zoma's side of the coin:
Why do you think that Elazar HaKappar says that pursuing honor takes one out of the world?*	Give three examples of how someone could be rich and happy, but not have money:
_____	1. _____
_____	_____
_____	_____
Why might he feel it is wrong to pursue honor?	2. _____
_____	_____
_____	_____
_____	3. _____
* The rabbis of his time would say things like "take one out of the world" when they meant "it's not good for the person."	_____
	_____

Now think about the two sides together. Answer the following questions.

1. Is a person who "pursues honor" (Rabbi Elazar HaKappar's thought) "happy with what he has in life" (Ben Zoma's thought)? Explain why or why not.

_____

_____

2. What is similar about the statements of Ben Zoma and Rabbi Elazar HaKappar? (In other words, what is the *same* about the "coin" they are on?)

_____

_____

3. How are these two statements different ideas about the same thought? Why are they on *different* sides of the same coin?

_____

_____

Here is the second מִשְׁנָה on honor.

6:4

This is the way of the [study] of Torah …	כָּךְ הִיא דַּרְכָּהּ שֶׁל תּוֹרָה...
Don't seek greatness for yourself and don't covet honor.	אַל תְּבַקֵּשׁ גְּדֻלָּה לְעַצְמְךָ וְאַל תַּחְמוֹד כָּבוֹד.
More than you've learned, do!	יוֹתֵר מִלִּמּוּדְךָ עֲשֵׂה
Don't desire the tables of kings, for your table is greater than theirs.	וְאַל תִּתְאַוֶּה לְשֻׁלְחָנָם שֶׁל שָׂרִים שֶׁשֻּׁלְחָנְךָ גָּדוֹל מִשֻּׁלְחָנָם
Your crown is grander than theirs.	וְכִתְרְךָ גָּדוֹל מִכִּתְרָם.

There's a well-known story in the Bible of someone who wanted greatness, coveted honor, and "desired the table of kings" but did not succeed. The same story tells of someone who did not pursue honor whose "crown became greater than kings," in the end.

 Read the verses below, which are from the Book of Esther. Then answer the two questions:

1. Who pursued honor but did not receive any?
2. Who did *not* seek honor but received it anyway?

ON THAT NIGHT THE KING COULDN'T SLEEP AND HE ORDERED THE BOOK OF RECORDS, THE CHRONICLES, TO BE BROUGHT. IT WAS READ TO THE KING.

IT WAS FOUND WRITTEN THAT MORDECHAI REPORTED AGAINST BIGTANA AND TERESH, TWO OF THE KING'S CHAMBERLAINS, THE KEEPERS OF THE DOOR, WHO WANTED TO KILL KING ACHASUERUS.

THE KING ASKED, "WHAT HONOR OR ADVANCEMENT WAS DONE FOR MORDECHAI BECAUSE OF THIS?"

THE KING'S SERVANTS SAID, "NOTHING WAS DONE FOR HIM."

THE KING ASKED, "WHO IS IN THE COURTYARD?" (HAMAN HAD COME TO THE OUTER COURTYARD OF THE ROYAL PALACE TO ASK THE KING TO HANG MORDECHAI ON THE TREE THAT HE HAD PREPARED FOR HIM.)

THE KING'S SERVANTS ANSWERED, "IT IS HAMAN STANDING IN THE COURTYARD."

THE KING SAID, "LET HIM COME IN."

HAMAN ENTERED AND THE KING SAID TO HIM, "WHAT SHOULD BE DONE FOR THE MAN WHOM THE KING WANTS TO HONOR?"

HAMAN THOUGHT TO HIMSELF, "WHO COULD THE KING WANT TO HONOR MORE THAN ME?"

SO HAMAN SAID TO THE KING, "FOR THE MAN THE KING WANTS TO HONOR LET ROYAL CLOTHING BE BROUGHT THAT THE KING HAS WORN AND A HORSE THE KING RIDES, ON THE HEAD OF WHICH A ROYAL CROWN IS PLACED.

"AND LET THIS CLOTHING AND HORSE BE DELIVERED TO THE HAND OF ONE OF THE KING'S MOST NOBLE PRINCES THAT HE MAY DRESS THE MAN

WHOM THE KING WANTS TO HONOR AND BRING HIM ON HORSEBACK THROUGH THE STREETS OF THE CITY AND SAY BEFORE HIM, 'THUS SHALL BE DONE TO THE MAN WHOM THE KING DELIGHTS TO HONOR.'"

THEN THE KING SAID TO HAMAN, "QUICKLY, TAKE THE CLOTHING AND THE HORSE, JUST LIKE YOU SAID, AND DO SO TO MORDECHAI THE JEW WHO SITS AT THE KING'S GATE.

"DO NOT LEAVE OUT ANYTHING FROM WHAT YOU SUGGESTED."

ESTHER 6:1–10

The person who pursued honor but lost it was _____

_____.

The person who did not pursue honor, but was honored was _____

_____.

Why or why not is this fair? _____

_____.

23

An Ending Thought from You

It is nice to be honored by others—to win a sports trophy, to have poetry or writing published in a school journal, to have someone say, "You're great!" In this chapter we read two selections from פִּרְקֵי אָבוֹת that warn against *pursuing* honor, for, as we saw with Haman, such an action often backfires.

How, then, do we achieve honor? Ben Zoma asks, "Who is honored?" He then answers himself: "A person who honors others."

- This week, what might you do to honor someone else?

  _____

  _____

- What honor might you get back in return?

  _____

  _____

A WISE PERSON OR A FOOL?

Seven things distinguish a fool and seven things distinguish a wise person.

שִׁבְעָה דְבָרִים בְּגֹלֶם
וְשִׁבְעָה בְּחָכָם.

The wise person does not speak in the presence of one who is wiser.

חָכָם אֵינוֹ מְדַבֵּר לִפְנֵי
מִי שֶׁגָּדוֹל מִמֶּנּוּ בְּחָכְמָה וּבְמִנְיָן.

The wise person does not interrupt when another is speaking.

וְאֵינוֹ נִכְנָס לְתוֹךְ
דִּבְרֵי חֲבֵרוֹ.

The wise person is not in a hurry to answer.

וְאֵינוֹ נִבְהָל
לְהָשִׁיב.

The wise person asks according to the subject, and answers according to the Law.

שׁוֹאֵל כָּעִנְיָן
וּמֵשִׁיב כַּהֲלָכָה.

The wise person speaks about the first matter first and the last matter last.

וְאוֹמֵר עַל רִאשׁוֹן רִאשׁוֹן
וְעַל אַחֲרוֹן אַחֲרוֹן.

גֹּלֶם	If there is something the wise person has not heard [and therefore does not know], the wise person says, "I have never heard [of it]."	וְעַל מַה שֶּׁלֹּא שָׁמַע
Shapeless mass or embryo (golem); the name of a very famous Jewish "monster" reportedly brought to life by a rabbi. Here it is translated as "fool."		אוֹמֵר לֹא שָׁמַעְתִּי.
	The wise person acknowledges what is true. The opposite of all these qualities is found in a fool.	וּמוֹדֶה עַל הָאֱמֶת.
		וְחִלּוּפֵיהֶן בְּגֹלֶם.

A Beginning Thought: A person's behavior tells a lot about his or her character.

It's not just what we say that matters, but also what we do.

- When we see someone admit to breaking a glass vase, to not telling the truth about finishing homework, or to forgetting to feed the dog, we might say that person has an *honest character*.
- When we see that a best friend never tells any of our secrets, we might say that person has a *trustworthy character*.
- When we see that a classmate never gets frustrated with long assignments, can sit and play with younger children for hours, or can put together a 1,000 piece puzzle, we might say that person has a *patient character*.

 A person's character tells us something steady and certain about him or her, either positive or negative. So, a person can be (fill in the blanks):

Honest ⟷ *Dishonest* | Loyal ⟷ _____

Trustworthy ⟷ *Untrustworthy* | Cheerful ⟷ _____

Patient ⟷ *Impatient* | _____ ⟷ _____

_____ ⟷ Cowardly

Behaviors Label Our Character

 With a partner, look at the comic strip below and then answer the questions:

1. Describe each person's behaviors and actions:

The brother	The sister

2. Based on those behaviors and actions, how would you describe each person's character?

The brother	The sister

How Does a Wise Person Behave?

We read in פִּרְקֵי אָבוֹת a list of seven **characteristics** of a wise person. According to this list, a "wise" person is not the same as a "smart" person.

 With a partner, read each of the **characteristics** on page 28 and match them by writing the letter in the blank space with the **behaviors** on page 29 that you might see from a wise person:

Characteristics

1. The wise person does not speak in the presence of one who is wiser. ____

2. The wise person does not interrupt when another is speaking. ____

3. The wise person is not in a hurry to answer. ____

4. The wise person asks according to the subject, and answers according to the Law. ____

5. The wise person speaks about the first matter first and the last matter last. ____

6. If there is something the wise person has not heard [and therefore does not know], the wise person says, "I have never heard [of it]." ____

7. The wise person acknowledges what is true. ____

---

characteristic
A specific quality in a person.

Behaviors

A. "I think it's important to first decide what we want to do. Then we can decide what time to leave."

B. "I've never heard about *pidyon haben*," Mrs. Pierson said. "But you raise an interesting question, Danielle. I think the cantor is in her office. Would you mind seeing if she can give you an answer? Then come back and tell us what you find out."

C. Dr. Snydman reached for the book on his desk that explained different medicines and proper doses. He checked for the correct amount to prescribe for his patient.

D. "Yes, it is true that we don't know where Moshe was buried. We read that in chapter 34 of Deuteronomy. Why do you think his burial place was kept a secret?"

E. At a national science fair, a teacher stood by her student's exhibit, next to the student. When someone asked a question about the display, the teacher said nothing, allowing the student who had done the research to answer.

F. Jessica thought the tour guide might have misquoted something, but she waited patiently until he was done speaking.

G. "But how many candles are we supposed to light?" asked Emily, thinking about *Havdalah*.
"At least two," Shai quickly replied, thinking about the beginning of Shabbat.
"One braided candle with at least two wicks," answered Rachel, thinking about *Havdalah*.

What Kind of Person Is the Opposite of "Wise"?

 פִּרְקֵי אָבוֹת tells us that "the opposite of all these qualities is found in a fool." With a partner, write down what the opposite behavior of each of these "wise characteristics" would be.

1. The wise person does not speak in the presence of one who is wiser.

   A fool _answers someone's question about stomach pains, even though a_ _real doctor is also in the room._

2. The wise person does not interrupt when another is speaking.

   A fool _____

   _____.

3. The wise person is not in a hurry to answer.

   A fool _____

   _____.

4. The wise person asks according to the subject, and answers according to the Law.

   A fool _____

   _____.

5. If there is something the wise person has not heard [and therefore does not know], the wise person says, "I have never heard [of it]."

   A fool _____

   _____.

6. The wise person speaks about the first matter first and the last matter last.

   A fool _____

   _____.

7. The wise person acknowledges what is true.

   A fool _____

   _____.

What Is a גֹּלֶם?

The Hebrew word גֹּלֶם translated here as "fool" is an interesting one. The word really means a "shapeless mass." At the time פִּרְקֵי אָבוֹת was written, people used the word to mean "something that is unfinished."

 Sit with three people and discuss the questions below.

1. How might a person's character be shapeless, or unfinished?

   _____

   _____

   _____

   _____

2. פִּרְקֵי אָבוֹת tells us that a גֹּלֶם (a shapeless, unfinished person) is the opposite of a wise person. Why do you think the rabbis thought that "shapeless and unfinished" might be the opposite of wise?

   _____

   _____

   _____

   _____

An Ending Thought from You

If a person's behavior gives us clues to his or her character, think about what this means for yourself.

- How would you describe your character? (Hint: If you're stuck for ideas, check out page 11.)

_____   _____

_____   _____

_____   _____

_____

- What behaviors do you show others that would give them clues about your character?

_____

_____

_____

_____

- Think about a character trait (a quality) you would like to develop in yourself. To do so, what behaviors might you consider experimenting with?

_____

_____

_____

_____

CONSEQUENCES

There are four kinds of **temperaments**:

אַרְבַּע מִדוֹת בַּדֵּעוֹת:

[One is] easy to anger, and easy to calm.
That one's gain is canceled by the loss.

נוֹחַ לִכְעוֹס וְנוֹחַ לִרְצוֹת.
יָצָא הֶפְסֵדוֹ בִּשְׂכָרוֹ.

[One is] hard to anger, and hard to calm.
That one's loss is canceled by the gain.

קָשֶׁה לִכְעוֹס וְקָשֶׁה לִרְצוֹת.
יָצָא שְׂכָרוֹ בְּהֶפְסֵדוֹ.

[One is] hard to anger and easy to calm.
The best way.

קָשֶׁה לִכְעוֹס וְנוֹחַ לִרְצוֹת.
חָסִיד.

The last is easy to anger and hard to calm.
The worst way.

נוֹחַ לִכְעוֹס וְקָשֶׁה לִרְצוֹת.
רָשָׁע.

> **temperament**
> General way in which a person handles emotions and approaches life.

A Beginning Thought: There are consequences to the way we handle our emotions.

At a very young age, we learned that our actions have consequences:

When we cried, someone came to see what we needed.

When we let go of the rattle, it fell from view.

When our cup tipped over, the juice inside dripped out.

 As we grew, we learned other consequences in life:

When we hit someone, she did not want to be our friend.

When we shared a toy, we made someone else happy.

A harder-to-learn lesson in life is finding out that how we handle our emotions also has consequences.

Getting Angry

Anger is a natural emotion. We get might get angry when we lose a game, someone is not fair, or we are disappointed. List two other reasons why people get angry.

1. _____

2. _____

The מִשְׁנָה from פִּרְקֵי אָבוֹת teaches that there are different consequences to our anger, depending on

- how hard or easy it was for our anger to erupt.
- how hard or easy it was for us to calm down.

With two or three classmates, consider the behaviors of four students who each faced the same situation while using a computer at school:

Each student wrote a one-page essay on the computer but forgot to save the document. Each student had started to print the essay when the computer froze. Each student reacted a little bit differently.

- Leah immediately got really angry but calmed down in about five minutes.
  What do you think other students thought about her behavior?

  _____

  _____

- Daniel did not get angry until it happened three times, but he held onto his anger for days and made a fuss about using the school computers each time after that.
  What do you think other students thought about his behavior?

  _____

  _____

- Emma did not get angry until it happened three times, but got over it quickly, laughing each time five minutes later about how silly it was that she again forgot to save her essay.
  What do you think other students thought about her behavior?

  _____

  _____

- Jonathan got angry immediately and held onto his anger for days, making a fuss about using the school computers each time after that.
  What do you think other students thought about his behavior?

  _____

  _____

How Long to Anger? How Long to Calm Down?

 Here's a story about a person who was provoked to anger. As you read it, think about both how long it took the man with no name to get angry and how long it took him to calm down. Then, with a partner, answer the questions that follow.

ONCE RABBI ELEAZAR, SON OF RABBI SIMEON, WAS COMING FROM MIGDAL GEDOR, FROM THE HOUSE OF HIS TEACHER. HE WAS RIDING LEISURELY ON HIS DONKEY BY THE RIVERSIDE AND WAS FEELING HAPPY BECAUSE HE HAD STUDIED MUCH TORAH.

THERE HE MET AN UGLY MAN WHO GREETED HIM: "שָׁלוֹם עָלֶיךָ, רַבִּי".

RABBI ELEAZAR DID NOT RETURN THE GREETING, BUT INSTEAD SAID TO THE MAN, "HOW UGLY YOU ARE! ARE ALL YOUR TOWNSPEOPLE AS UGLY AS YOU?"

THE MAN SAID, "I DO NOT KNOW, BUT GO AND SAY TO THE CRAFTSMAN WHO MADE ME, 'HOW UGLY IS THE VESSEL WHICH YOU HAVE MADE.'"

WHEN RABBI ELEAZAR REALIZED THAT HE HAD DONE WRONG, HE GOT DOWN FROM THE DONKEY AND BOWED DOWN BEFORE THE MAN AND SAID TO HIM, "PLEASE, PLEASE FORGIVE ME!"

THE MAN ANSWERED, "I WILL NOT FORGIVE YOU UNTIL YOU GO TO THE CRAFTSMAN WHO MADE ME AND SAY TO HIM, 'HOW UGLY IS THE VESSEL WHICH YOU HAVE MADE.'"

RABBI ELEAZAR WALKED BEHIND THE MAN UNTIL HE REACHED THE RABBI'S NATIVE CITY. WHEN THE TOWNSPEOPLE CAME OUT, THEY GREETED RABBI ELEAZAR WITH THE WORDS, "שָׁלוֹם עָלֶיךָ, רַבִּי רַבִּי, מוֹרִי מוֹרִי".

THE MAN ASKED THE TOWNSPEOPLE, "WHOM ARE YOU CALLING THESE NAMES?"

THEY ANSWERED, "THE PERSON WHO IS WALKING WITH YOU."

THEN THE MAN SAID, "IF THIS PERSON IS A TEACHER, MAY THERE NOT BE ANY MORE LIKE HIM IN ISRAEL!"

THE PEOPLE THEN ASKED THE MAN, "WHY?"

THE MAN TOLD THE PEOPLE WHAT RABBI ELEAZAR HAD DONE.

שָׁלוֹם עָלֶיךָ
רַבִּי

"Peace to you, my teacher" (*Shalom alecha rahbi*).

שָׁלוֹם עָלֶיךָ
רַבִּי רַבִּי
מוֹרִי מוֹרִי

"Peace to you, my rabbi my rabbi, my teacher my teacher" (*Shalom alecha rahbi rahbi, mori mori*).

THE TOWNSPEOPLE SAID TO THE MAN, "BUT YOU SHOULD FORGIVE HIM, FOR HE IS A PERSON WHO KNOWS A LOT OF TORAH."

THE MAN ANSWERED, "FOR YOUR SAKES I WILL FORGIVE HIM, BUT ONLY ON THE CONDITION THAT HE DOES NOT ACT THE SAME WAY IN THE FUTURE."

SOON AFTER THIS, RABBI ELEAZAR, SON OF RABBI SIMEON, ENTERED THE HOUSE OF STUDY AND TAUGHT:

A PERSON SHOULD ALWAYS BE AS GENTLE AS THE REED,

AND LET HIM NEVER BE AS UNYIELDING AS THE CEDAR.

B. TALMUD *TAANIT* 20A

1. Was the man quick to get angry or slow to get angry? _____ Which part of the story supports your answer? _____

   _____

   _____

2. Was the man quick to calm down, or did it take a long time? _____ Which part of the story supports your answer? _____

   _____

   _____

3. For the man, what were the consequences of the way he handled his emotions? _____

   _____

   _____

4. What does the verse from פִּרְקֵי אָבוֹת say is the consequence of someone who has this kind of **temperament**? _____

_____

_____

5. Explain why you agree or disagree with the opinion expressed in פִּרְקֵי אָבוֹת. You may use examples other than the text. _____

_____

_____

_____

Thinking about Other Emotions

The way we handle our emotions affects the way others think about us. With a partner, think about each example below and fill in the blanks.

1. David is homesick at camp and complains to anyone who passes his cabin.

   • Identify the emotion. _____

   • What might be the consequences of David's actions? _____

   _____

2. Naomi loves her grandmother very much and smiles a lot thinking about the good times they have together.

   • Identify the emotion. _____

   • What might be the consequences of Naomi's actions? _____

   _____

3. Sam is really nervous about his bar mitzvah and gets angry quickly at his family. However, each time he goes to his room to calm down afterward.

   • Identify the emotion. _____

   • What might be the consequences of Sam's actions?_____

   _____

An Ending Thought from You

One of the things we learned earlier about Ben Zoma was that he believed a mighty person was one who controlled his or her emotions. Ben Zoma and the author of the מִשְׁנָה we studied in this chapter both understood that people get angry, just as they might become happy, or sad, or embarrassed. Emotions are an important part of our lives. But these two rabbis wanted us to know that how we handle our emotions has consequences for us.

   • Think of a time when you had a strong emotional reaction and write about it here.

   _____

   _____

   • What were the consequences of how you handled your emotions?

   _____

   _____

   • How would you want to react in the future to the same situation? Would you react in the same way? Why or why not?

   _____

   _____

THE LITTLE THINGS IN LIFE

3:4

Rabbi Chanina ben Chachinai would say,

    "One who spends the night awake

    or who goes on a journey alone

    or who turns one's mind to useless thoughts

sins against one's own soul."

רַבִּי חֲנִינָא בֶּן חֲכִינַאי אוֹמֵר

הַנֵּעוֹר בַּלַּיְלָה

וְהַמְהַלֵּךְ בַּדֶּרֶךְ יְחִידִי

וּמְפַנֶּה לִבּוֹ לְבַטָלָה

הֲרֵי זֶה מִתְחַיֵּב בְּנַפְשׁוֹ.

3:10

Rabbi Dosa ben Harkinas used to say,

רַבִּי דּוֹסָא בֶּן הָרְכִּינַס אוֹמֵר

"Morning sleep,

שֵׁנָה שֶׁל שַׁחֲרִית

midday wine,

וְיַיִן שֶׁל צָהֳרַיִם

children's talk,

וְשִׂיחַת הַיְלָדִים

and attendance at the meeting places of the ignorant—

וִישִׁיבַת בָּתֵּי כְנֵסִיּוֹת שֶׁל עַמֵּי הָאָרֶץ

all will take a person out of this world."

מוֹצִיאִין אֶת הָאָדָם מִן הָעוֹלָם.

A Beginning Thought: The little things in life can make a big difference.

We might almost believe that the rabbis of פִּרְקֵי אָבוֹת and our parents have been talking across the centuries! Parents often tell their children what to do and what is and is not appropriate, simply because they feel that the little things we do in life can make a big difference to our current happiness and future success. Read the list below and check off the statements you have heard from at least one of your parents, or from another adult, throughout your life. There is room, also, to add other things you have heard.

___ Look both ways before crossing the street.

___ No TV before your homework is done.

___ Be home before your curfew.

___ Don't walk there unless you have a friend with you.

___ Those video games rot a person's mind!

___ Don't talk to strangers.

___ You're sleeping the day away!

___ Your teacher won't want you to quote a statement from a chatroom for your research paper.

___ _____

_____

What Does It Mean?

These two verses from פִּרְקֵי אָבוֹת tell us what two rabbis who lived almost 2,000 years ago thought were important pieces of advice.

 Work in groups to complete the chart on the next page. Think about examples you may know from the news or from your own lives. In the last box, place a check (✔) if you think the advice is still good today.

What it says in פִּרְקֵי אָבוֹת	An example from today	Why this can cause problems for a person	✔
Spending the night awake	Staying up until after 1:00 a.m. to watch TV		☐
Going on a journey alone			☐
Turning one's mind to useless thoughts	Worrying about passing a test, rather than studying for it		☐
Morning sleep			☐
Midday wine			☐
Children's talk	Talking on the phone for hours about a cute boy or girl		☐
Attending the meeting places of the ignorant	Hanging out with kids who regularly cut school		☐

What Do Others Think?

 Survey four people to find out what they think are three things that create problems for teenagers. Be sure to include at least two adults in your survey.

Name _____   Name _____

1._____   1._____

2._____   2._____

3._____   3._____

Name _____   Name _____

1._____   1._____

2._____   2._____

3._____   3._____

Read over all the advice given to you by others. Circle the three thoughts that you think are most important to watch out for.

In the News

By carefully reading the news, we can find examples of the little things in life that make a big difference. For example, in a news article with the headline **CHILD HURT IN BIKE ACCIDENT** you might find that the youngster thought it was not cool to wear a bike helmet and so was hospitalized with a concussion after falling off his bike. You could therefore conclude that it's important to wear a bike helmet whenever you ride a bike.

Look in your local newspaper or on the Internet for three news articles from which you can find advice for life today. Copy each headline, and write what you can learn from each.

The headline:

_____

What you can learn from the article:

_____

_____

The headline:

_____

What you can learn from the article:

_____

_____

The headline:

_____

What you can learn from the article:

_____

_____

An Ending Thought from You

In this chapter, you read and heard a lot of advice from other people. Each piece of advice was about the "little things in life" that can make a big difference. Think for a moment about the "little things" that have made a big difference in your life that you'd like to share with a younger brother or sister, cousin, or friend. Then, write your thoughts here:

 "Little thing" #1 _____

_____

"Little thing" #2 _____

_____

"Little thing" #3 _____

_____

Unit Wrap-Up

פִּרְקֵי אָבוֹת on Character

If I am not for myself, who will be for me?

When we focus on ourselves, we focus on our "character," including who we are, how we behave, and the things that are personally important to us. This unit has focused on several aspects of a person's character, including:

Emotions
- Happiness
- Anger
- Envy

Temperament
- How easily a person gets angry
- How easily a person calms down

Character traits
- A person's good name
- Self-control (remember the answer to "Who is mighty?")
- Honor
- Wisdom
- Satisfaction with what one has (remember the answer to "Who is rich?")

How would you describe your own character

What about your character would you like to improve?

_____   _____

_____   _____

_____   _____

_____   _____

UNIT II

IF I AM FOR MYSELF ALONE, WHAT AM I?

HILLEL ASKS, "IF?"

He [Hillel] used to say,

"If I am not for myself,
who will be for me?

And if I am for myself alone,
then what am I?

And if not now, when?"

הוּא הָיָה אוֹמֵר

אִם אֵין אֲנִי לִי
מִי לִי?

וּכְשֶׁאֲנִי לְעַצְמִי
מָה אֲנִי?

וְאִם לֹא עַכְשָׁו אֵימָתַי?

A Beginning Thought: We have to take care of ourselves, *and* we have an obligation to help others.

A young child is self-centered.

If her parents are around, she clamours for their attention.

She loves one-on-one snuggling in an adult's lap.

She may have trouble understanding that other people have needs that compete with her own.

However, as the child grows older, she learns that while she can depend on others, she also has to take care of herself.

With a partner, think about some very young children you know. Make a list of the things you see them doing independently.

getting dressed _____   _____

_____   _____

_____   _____

_____   _____

_____   _____

_____   _____

Then, write down some reasons why you think young children learn to begin taking care of themselves.

_____

_____

_____

_____

If I Am Not for Myself, Who Will Be for Me?

Hillel was a rabbi who lived more than 2,000 years ago. The Talmud has quite a few stories about him, as well as some of his teachings. In this chapter, we will be looking at one of his teachings, which you may already know as a song.

אָם אֵין אֲנִי לִי מִי לִי?

וּכְשֶׁאֲנִי לְעַצְמִי מָה אֲנִי?

וְאָם לֹא עַכְשָׁו אֵימָתַי?

The first line of this מִשְׁנָה asks, "If I am not for myself, who will be for me?" In other words, when we feel good about ourselves and advocate for what we need in life, then others will "be for us" as well. There's an old Greek story of a poor farmer who was taking his produce to the market. One wheel on his crickety old cart got stuck in the mud. He did not think he had the power to push his cart out of the mud, and so he sat for a really long time, crying. Finally, he got up and put his shoulder to the cart and encouraged his donkey to pull. Not much happened at first, but then a Greek god came and helped the man push his cart out. As he headed off, with the thanks of the poor man, the god said, "Heaven helps those who help themselves."

 With a partner, answer these questions:

1. What did the man in the story do to show that he was "for himself"? _____

_____

2. When the man showed that he was willing to try and take care of himself, what

   extra help did he get? _____

_____

3. What does this story have to do with the first line of Hillel's saying, "If I am not for myself, who will be for me?" _____

_____

4. What two stories from your own lives, or perhaps from a TV show or movie, illustrate a similar situation?

    • _____

    _____

    • _____

    _____

Complete this activity individually.

1. Make a list of six great things about yourself.

    _____   _____

    _____   _____

    _____   _____

2. Now describe a time when you had to show that you were "for yourself." Perhaps you had to advocate for something you really, really wanted. Perhaps you decided to try and do something that others thought you might not do well. When were *you* "for yourself"?

    _____

    _____

    _____

    _____

3. Who are your personal "cheerleaders"? That is, who are the people who stand behind you through thick and thin? Who helps you feel good about yourself?

_____   _____

_____   _____

_____   _____

_____   _____

4. Finally, describe at least one time in your life when someone else stepped in to make things a bit easier for you after you showed that you were "for yourself."

_____

_____

_____

_____

Join together with 3 or 4 other people and share some of the answers you wrote above. You will each have to decide which memories and writings are private, and which you are willing to share.

As a group, decide whether you agree or disagree with the first part of Hillel's statement: "If I am not for myself, who will be for me?"

_____

_____

_____

_____

_____

And If Am for Myself Alone, Then What Am I?

We can understand Hillel's second question in at least two ways. Take a look at two different kinds of comments about people:

List 1	List 2
"Jeremy's such a snob! Unless he thinks you wear the 'right clothes,' he doesn't want you near him."	"Matt donated 20 precent of his bar mitzvah gift money to the homeless shelter his synagogue supports."
"Jonah gave candy to everyone who said they'd vote for him in the class election. He also 'dissed' the other candidates who were running."	"Alex helped me study for my test."
"Sue is so self-centered!"	"Ali can't come with us. On Tuesdays she always visits her grandmother after school."

With a partner, read through both lists, and then answer these following questions.

1. In which list are people "only for themselves"? ☐ List 1 ☐ List 2
    How would you answer the question "What am I?" for the people in the list you checked off? (Hint: use some adjectives.)

    _____

    _____

2. Look at List 2. Do these people like being:
    ☐ only for themselves?
    ☐ for themselves and others?
    ☐ only for others?

Explain why you checked off the answer you did.

_____

_____

Hillel wants us to realize that it *is* important to take care of ourselves. But he also wants us to realize that it's important not to be *only* for ourselves. We need to be "for" other people, as well. His question, "What am I?" is a rhetorical question. This means that Hillel does not expect a listing of answers. Rather, he is making the point that it is *not* good to be only for ourselves. We need to look beyond our own issues and figure out how to help others, too.

 Whom do you know who takes seriously the **rhetorical** question, "And if I am for myself alone, what am I?" This person would not only be for him- or herself, but also would do things for others—and this person could even be you! List three things this person has done to be "for others."

_____

_____

If Not Now, When?

Hillel wants us to know that it's important to act now, not later. The Talmud tells this story about a different rabbi who regretted not acting right away:

> NACHUM OF GAMZU WAS CARRYING A GIFT OF FOOD TO HIS FATHER-IN-LAW'S HOUSE WHEN HE MET A MAN COVERED WITH BOILS. THE MAN SAID, "GIVE ME PART OF WHAT YOU HAVE WITH YOU."
> NACHUM SAID, "WHEN I COME BACK."
> WHEN NACHUM CAME BACK, THE MAN WAS DEAD. NACHUM SAID, "MAY MY EYES, WHICH SAW YOU WHEN I DID NOT GIVE, BECOME BLIND. MAY MY HANDS, WHICH DID NOT REACH OUT TO YOU, BE CUT OFF. MAY MY LEGS, WHICH DID NOT HURRY TO GIVE TO YOU, BE BROKEN."
> AND IT HAPPENED TO HIM, JUST LIKE HE SAID.
>
> J. TALMUD *PEI-AH* VIII, 9, F. 21B, LINE 39

rhetorical
Used to describe a question or statement that does not need a response. The person asking it is doing it to make a point and usually believes that there is only one correct answer to the question, and that the people listening know it too.

While this rabbi took "And if not now, when?" to the extreme, the story shows us the uncertainty of life. If we do not act now, we may not get another chance.

An Ending Thought from You

In his famous verse from פִּרְקֵי אָבוֹת, Hillel is saying that we have to stand up for ourselves, but we cannot be too self centered; we also have to take care of others. Most important, Hillel reminds us that we should not wait to take action.

- In the next few days, think of this verse and put it into action. Then, answer the questions below.

    1. When did you need to be "for yourself alone"?

    _____

    _____

    2. When were you not only "for yourself alone"?

    _____

    _____

    3. When did you act quickly?

    _____

    _____

- Do you think Hillel is right? _____

    Explain. _____

    _____

IS IT MINE OR IS IT YOURS?

There are four kinds of human beings.

אַרְבַּע מִדּוֹת בָּאָדָם.

One says,
"What is mine is mine
and what is yours is yours."
That is the usual kind,
although some say that
is the **Sodom kind**.

הָאוֹמֵר
שֶׁלִּי שֶׁלִּי
וְשֶׁלְּךָ שֶׁלָּךְ
זוֹ מִדָּה בֵּינוֹנִית.
וְיֵשׁ אוֹמְרִים
זוֹ מִדַּת סְדוֹם.

[The one who says,]
"What is mine is yours
and what is yours is mine"
is simple-minded.

שֶׁלִּי שֶׁלָּךְ
וְשֶׁלְּךָ שֶׁלִּי
עַם הָאָרֶץ.

Sodom kind

This refers to the kind of behavior shown by the people of Sodom and Gomorrah, the two towns God destroyed (see Genesis 18–19).

[The one who says,]
"What is mine is yours
and what is yours is yours"
is the best way.

שֶׁלִּי שֶׁלָּךְ
וְשֶׁלְּךָ שֶׁלָּךְ
חָסִיד.

[And the one who says,]
"What is mine is mine
and what is yours is mine"
is the worst way.

שֶׁלְּךָ שֶׁלִּי
וְשֶׁלִּי שֶׁלִּי
רָשָׁע.

A Beginning Thought: People are often judged by how they share and by how they respect the property of others.

In the last chapter we looked at a well-known statement of Hillel:

> IF I AM NOT FOR MYSELF, WHO WILL BE FOR ME? AND IF I AM FOR MYSELF
> ALONE, WHAT AM I? AND IF NOT NOW, WHEN?

Hillel was concerned about people both taking care of themselves *and* taking care of the needs of others. The מִשְׁנָה in this chapter focuses on property—our own and that of others.

Sharing with Others

Imagine that some friends decide to have a party together. To keep costs down, everyone agrees to bring some food.

• With a partner, read about four of the friends and then decide which part of the verse from פִּרְקֵי אָבוֹת each one matches:

1. Josh brought some candy. He kept it to himself. He also ate freely from the candy and cookies that others brought with them.

   A. What is mine is mine and what is yours is yours.

2. Anna brought some chips. She held onto the bag all night and did not offer any to the others. She also did not take any food that the others brought.

   B. What is mine is yours and what is yours is mine.

3. Steve brought vegetables and dip. He put his platter on the table and told others to help themselves. He also ate what others brought.

   C. What is mine is yours and what is yours is yours.

4. Barbara brought nachos and cheese sauce. She placed her bowls on the table and shared with everyone else. She did not eat anything that anyone else had brought.

   D. What is mine is mine and what is yours is mine.

- Now think about each of these youngsters. How might you label the behavior of each person?

  1. We think that Josh's behavior was _____.

     We would/would not want to be Josh's friends because _____

     _____.

  2. We think that Anna's behavior was _____.

     We would/would want to be Anna's friends because _____

     _____.

  3. We think that Steve's behavior was _____.

     We would/would want to be Steve's friends because _____

     _____.

  4. We think that Barbara's behavior was _____.

     We would/would want to be Barbara's friends because _____

     _____.

- Recall that in our verse of פִּרְקֵי אָבוֹת, the rabbis gave each of these people a label. Read each one and check off those you agree with.
     ☐ Josh: The worst way.
     ☐ Anna: The usual kind.
     ☐ Steve: Simple-minded.
     ☐ Barbara: The best way.

- If you were having a party and you could invite only one of these people, who would it be? _____

  Why? _____

  _____

  _____

The Legend of the Two Brothers

 Read and discuss this story with a partner. Then answer the questions on the next page.

THERE WERE TWO BROTHERS, EACH A FARMER, WHO LIVED NEAR EACH OTHER ON OPPOSITE SIDES OF A HILL. ONE BROTHER WAS MARRIED AND HAD SEVERAL CHILDREN. THE OTHER BROTHER WAS UNMARRIED AND LIVED ALONE.

ONE YEAR THE WHEAT HARVEST WAS ESPECIALLY GOOD. THE MARRIED BROTHER LOOKED AT HIS CROP, THOUGHT OF HIS GOOD FORTUNE, AND SAID, "GOD HAS BEEN GOOD TO ME. I HAVE A WIFE AND CHILDREN AND MORE WHEAT THAN I NEED. MY BROTHER, HOWEVER, LIVES ALONE. HE HAS NO CHILDREN WHO WILL TAKE CARE OF HIM IN HIS OLD AGE. IT MUST BE HARD FOR HIM." SO THE MARRIED BROTHER DECIDED TO TAKE SOME OF HIS CROP AND ADD IT TO HIS BROTHER'S HARVEST ON THE OTHER SIDE OF THE HILL.

THE SAME NIGHT, THE UNMARRIED BROTHER LOOKED AT HIS CROP, THOUGHT OF HIS GOOD FORTUNE, AND SAID, "GOD HAS BEEN GOOD TO ME. I LIVE ALONE AND HAVE MORE WHEAT THAN I NEED. MY BROTHER, HOWEVER, HAS A WIFE AND CHILDREN. IT MUST BE HARD FOR HIM." SO THE UNMARRIED BROTHER DECIDED TO TAKE SOME OF HIS CROP AND ADD IT TO HIS BROTHER'S HARVEST ON THE OTHER SIDE OF THE HILL.

EACH BROTHER WAITED UNTIL THE FULL MOON WAS HIGH IN THE SKY, TOOK A LARGE WHEELBARROW FILLED WITH WHEAT, AND WALKED TOWARD HIS BROTHER'S FARM. AT THE TOP OF THE HILL, EACH MAN STOPPED AND SAW THE OTHER. IN AN INSTANT THEY UNDERSTOOD....

1. What do you think the two brothers understood?

_____

_____

2. Which of these phrases from our verse of פִּרְקֵי אָבוֹת does this story illustrate?
   ☐ What is mine is mine and what is yours is yours.
   ☐ What is mine is yours and what is yours is mine.
   ☐ What is mine is yours and what is yours is yours.
   ☐ What is mine is mine and what is yours is mine.

3. Why did you check that particular phrase?

_____

_____

How We Judge Others

The beginning thought in this chapter was:

PEOPLE ARE OFTEN JUDGED BY HOW THEY SHARE
AND BY HOW THEY RESPECT THE PROPERTY OF OTHERS.

☐ What is mine is mine and what is yours is yours.

Does this person share well?_____

Does this person respect the property of others? _____

Do you judge that this person is the "usual kind?"_____

Explain. _____

☐ What is mine is yours and what is yours is mine.

Does this person share well?_____

Does this person respect the property of others?_____

Do you judge that this person is simple-minded?_____

Explain. _____

☐ What is mine is yours and what is yours is yours.

Does this person share well?_____

Does this person respect the property of others?_____

Do you judge that this person is the best? _____

Explain. _____

☐ What is mine is mine and what is yours is mine.

Does this person share well?_____

Does this person respect the property of others?_____

Do you judge that this person is the worst? _____

Explain. _____

An Ending Thought from You

Take a moment and think about how you behave with your friends.

- How well do you share what you have with them?

  _____

  _____

- How well do you respect their property?

  _____

  _____

- How do you judge your own behavior?

  _____

  _____

HONOR AND RESPECT

---

associate

The Hebrew word is חָבֵר *(chaver)*, or friend. The translator used the word "associate" to mean someone who is equal to you (for example, a business associate).

---

reverence

Respect. The Hebrew word, מוֹרָא *(morah)*, is translated as "respect" the other times it is used here. The translator wanted to vary his word usage, so he substituted "reverence" in this phrase.

Rabbi Elazar ben Shamua would say,

רַבִּי אֶלְעָזָר בֶּן שַׁמּוּעַ אוֹמֵר

"Let the honor of your student be as dear to you as your own.

יְהִי כְבוֹד תַּלְמִידְךָ
חָבִיב עָלֶיךָ כְּשֶׁלָּךְ

Let the honor of your **associate** be equal to the respect due to your teacher.

וּכְבוֹד חֲבֵרְךָ
כְּמוֹרָא רַבָּךְ

Let the respect due to your teacher
be equivalent to the **reverence** due to God."

וּמוֹרָא רַבָּךְ
כְּמוֹרָא שָׁמָיִם.

A Beginning Thought: Those who teach us, and those who learn from us, deserve our respect.

 • Almost everyone remembers a favorite teacher. Who is yours? _____

_____

• Think back and describe what you liked about this person. _____

_____

• How did you show this teacher your respect? _____

_____

Respect

This מִשְׁנָה from פִּרְקֵי אָבוֹת discusses the honor and respect of *your* students, *your* "associates," *your* teachers, and God.

With a partner, reread the verse and decide to whom Rabbi Elazar ben Shamua is speaking when he says

• your student.

• your associate.

• your teacher.

We think that Rabbi Elazar is speaking to _____

when he says "your student, your associate, and your teacher" because _____

_____

_____

Respect Due to Teachers

Jewish tradition is very clear about the respect due to teachers. In the מִשְׁנָה we find this information:

> IF A PERSON GOES LOOKING FOR PROPERTY LOST BY HIS FATHER AND PROPERTY LOST BY HIS TEACHER, HIS TEACHER'S HAS PRIORITY OVER HIS FATHER'S BECAUSE HIS FATHER BROUGHT HIM INTO THIS WORLD, BUT HIS TEACHER, WHO TAUGHT HIM WISDOM, BRINGS HIM INTO THE WORLD-TO-COME....
>
> IF HIS FATHER AND HIS TEACHER CARRY A HEAVY BURDEN, HE MUST HELP HIS TEACHER FIRST AND THEN HIS FATHER.
>
> IF HIS FATHER AND HIS TEACHER WERE KIDNAPPED, HE MUST RANSOM HIS TEACHER FIRST AND THEN HIS FATHER.
>
> MISHNAH *BAVA M'TZIA* 2:11

 Work in a small group to read and understand this מִשְׁנָה.

1. Under what three circumstances does this מִשְׁנָה say a teacher has priority over a parent?

   _____

   _____

   _____

2. According to this מִשְׁנָה, *why* does a teacher have priority over a parent? Use your own words to explain.

   _____

   _____

   _____

3. Why would wisdom give a person a chance to experience a better world, a "world-to-come"?

_____

_____

_____

4. Do you agree with this מִשְׁנָה? Explain your reasoning (you might agree with one part but not with another).

_____

_____

_____

_____

5. In what circumstances would *you* say that a parent has priority over a teacher?

_____

_____

_____

_____

• Share your answer to the last question as a class.

Reverence Due to God

What does it mean to revere or respect God? These students offer you some possible answers.

I RESPECT GOD WHEN I REMEMBER NOT TO SWEAR USING GOD'S NAME.

I REVERE GOD WHEN I DO MY BEST.

I AM RESPECTFUL TO GOD WHEN I PRAY.

I TRY TO BEHAVE TOWARD OTHERS IN A WAY THAT GOD MIGHT BEHAVE.

I RESPECT GOD WHEN I REMEMBER THAT I AM CREATED בְּצֶלֶם אֱלֹהִים (B'TZELEM ELOHIM; IN THE IMAGE OF GOD).

With your partner, use these thoughts as well as your own to think about what the following means in real life: *Let the respect due to your teacher be equivalent to the reverence due to God.* How might students in your school show teachers this kind of respect?

_____

_____

_____

_____

Respect Goes Both Ways!

In this story from the Talmud, a student respects his teachers so much that he is willing to put his life in danger. Also in this story, the teachers respect their student so much that they break the laws of Shabbat to help him.

HILLEL THE ELDER WAS A POOR MAN. HE WORKED EVERY DAY AND EARNED ONLY HALF A DINAR. HE GAVE HALF OF THIS TO THE GUARD AT THE HOUSE OF STUDY TO PAY FOR HIS LESSONS AND USED THE OTHER HALF TO SUPPORT HIMSELF AND HIS FAMILY.

ONE FRIDAY NIGHT [BEFORE SHABBAT BEGAN] HILLEL EARNED NO MONEY, AND THE GUARD AT THE HOUSE OF STUDY WOULD NOT PERMIT HIM TO ENTER. HILLEL CLIMBED UP TO THE ROOF AND PUT HIS HEAD AGAINST THE SKYLIGHT, WHERE HE COULD HEAR THE WORDS SPOKEN BY THE RABBIS SHEMAIYAH AND AVTALYON. AS HE LAY ON THE ROOF, HEAVY SNOW BEGAN TO FALL ON HIM. BUT HILLEL REMAINED IN HIS PLACE ALL NIGHT.

THE NEXT MORNING [ON SHABBAT], SHEMAIYAH SAID TO AVTALYON, "THIS HOUSE IS LIGHT EVERY DAY, BUT TODAY IT IS DARK. IS IT CLOUDY OUTSIDE?"

THEY LOOKED UP AND SAW THE SHAPE OF A MAN IN THE SKYLIGHT. THEY CLIMBED TO THE ROOF AND FOUND HILLEL, COVERED WITH SNOW AND ALMOST FROZEN TO DEATH. THEY CARRIED HIM DOWN, BATHED HIM AND PUT OILS ON HIM, AND PLACED HIM NEAR THE FIRE. [NOTE: ALL THESE ACTIONS ARE AGAINST THE MITZVOT OF SHABBAT].

AND THEY SAID, "THIS MAN IS WORTHY OF BREAKING THE MITZVOT OF SHABBAT!"

B. TALMUD *YOMA* 35B

1. With a partner, discuss the following:
- The respect that you think that Hillel showed his teachers
- The respect that you think the teachers showed Hillel

2. Now discuss how respect can go both ways by answering the questions below:

A report was due today, but Joanie left it on the kitchen table.

If the teacher considered "Let the honor of your student be as dear to you as your own," what might he say to Joanie in this situation? _____

_____

_____

If Joanie considered "Let the respect due to your teacher be equivalent to the reverence due to God," what might she say to her teacher? _____

_____

_____

Sam was pretty sure that his teacher made a mistake when grading his test.

If Sam considered "Let the respect due to your teacher be equivalent to the reverence due to God," what might he say to his teacher? _____

_____

_____

If the teacher considered "Let the honor of your student be as dear to you as your own," what might she say to Sam in this situation? _____

_____

_____

Jon and some other students needed to write a report together, but his classmates were not doing their share of the work.

If Jon considered "Let the honor of your associate [your classmate] be equal to the respect due to your teacher," what might he say to his classmates in this situation? _____

_____

If Jon considered "Let the respect due to your teacher be equivalent to the reverence due to God," what might he say to his teacher? _____

_____

_____

If the teacher considered "Let the honor of your student be as dear to you as your own," what might he say to Jon or to the rest of the group in this situation? _____

_____

_____

An Ending Thought from You

Think of a situation in school that has been on your mind. Depending on the situation, answer one, two, or all three of the questions below.

- How might you consider "Let the honor of your student be as dear to you as your own," in solving the situation?

  _____

  _____

- How might you consider "Let the honor of your associate [classmate] be equal to the respect due to your teacher"?

  _____

  _____

- How might you consider "Let the respect due to your teacher be equivalent to the reverence due to God"?

  _____

  _____

BEING A GOOD FRIEND

Rabbi Shimon ben Elazar said,

רַבִּי שִׁמְעוֹן בֶּן אֶלְעָזָר אוֹמֵר

"When your friend becomes angry,
don't try to calm him.

אַל תְּרַצֶּה אֶת חֲבֵרְךָ
בִּשְׁעַת כַּעֲסוֹ.

When he is recently **bereaved**,
don't try to comfort him.

וְאַל תְּנַחֲמֵהוּ
בְּשָׁעָה שֶׁמֵּתוֹ מֻטָּל לְפָנָיו.

When he is about to make an oath,
don't ask him questions.

וְאַל תִּשְׁאַל לוֹ
בִּשְׁעַת נִדְרוֹ.

Just after he has been **disgraced**,
don't try to see him."

וְאַל תִּשְׁתַּדֵּל לִרְאוֹתוֹ
בִּשְׁעַת קַלְקָלָתוֹ.

bereaved
A person who is sad that someone he or she loved has died.

disgraced
A person who feels shame or who has lost honor. A disgraced person often feels embarrassed.

A Beginning Thought: Being a friend—a good friend—is hard work.

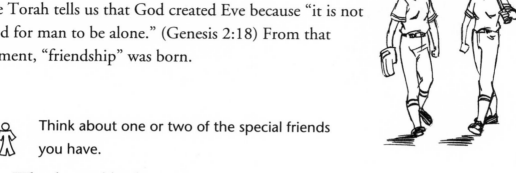

The Torah tells us that God created Eve because "it is not good for man to be alone." (Genesis 2:18) From that moment, "friendship" was born.

Think about one or two of the special friends you have.

• Why do you like that person? _____

_____

_____

• What is really special about your friendship?_____

_____

_____

• What are some things that can make it hard to be a friend? _____

_____

_____

• What do you do to make the friendship last? _____

_____

_____

Is Shimon ben Elazar Correct?

 Work in a group of three or four students to think about the advice of Shimon ben Elazar by filling in the chart that follows. As you work, decide whether you agree or disagree with him and be ready to explain your reasons to your partners.

	When your friend becomes angry	When your friend is bereaved	When your friend makes an oath	When your friend is disgraced
Give an example of why or how this might happen to your friend.				
Tell what Shimon ben Elazar says you should *not* do when this happens.				
Explain what might be the consequence of doing it anyway.				
Explain why you agree or disagree with the advice of Shimon ben Elazar.				

When Your Friend Becomes Angry, Don't Try to Calm Him.

The Book of Numbers (in Hebrew, בְּמִדְבַּר) tells how Moses sent twelve men to spy out the land of Canaan. Two of the men, Joshua and Caleb, felt confident that the Israelites could go and "gain possession" of the land. But the other ten told the Israelites that the people living there were stronger and larger than them. "We looked like grasshoppers," they said. As a result of this report, the Israelites cried out and said, "If only we had died in the land of Egypt, or if only we might die in this wilderness! … Let us head back to Egypt!" Moses and Aaron fell on their faces before the Israelites. Joshua and Caleb tore their clothes and pleaded with the people:

"IF *ADONAI* IS PLEASED WITH US, WE WILL BE BROUGHT INTO THAT LAND, A LAND FLOWING WITH MILK AND HONEY, AND IT WILL BE GIVEN TO US. DO NOT REBEL AGAINST *ADONAI*. DO NOT FEAR THE PEOPLE OF THE COUNTRY, FOR THEY ARE OUR PREY…. *ADONAI* IS WITH US. HAVE NO FEAR OF THEM!"

AS THE PEOPLE GOT READY TO THROW STONES AT THEIR LEADERS, GOD'S PRESENCE APPEARED AT THE TENT OF MEETING. *ADONAI* SAID TO MOSES, "HOW LONG WILL THIS PEOPLE REJECT ME? HOW LONG WILL THEY HAVE NO FAITH IN ME IN SPITE OF ALL THE SIGNS THAT I HAVE DONE IN THEIR MIDST? I WILL STRIKE THEM WITH DISEASE AND I WILL DISOWN THEM. I WILL MAKE YOU A NATION MORE NUMEROUS THAN THEY!"

NUMBERS 13:30–14:12

Working with a partner, fill out the charts that follow.

In this story, who became angry?	Who tried to calm down the person or group? How?	Did it seem to work?	What specific advice might Shimon ben Elazar have given in this situation?

Moses did try to calm God down. As you read what Moses said, think about his strategy and whether you feel it had a chance of working with God

What Moses said	Notes from you about Moses' strategy
"WHEN THE EGYPTIANS, FROM WHOM YOU BROUGHT OUT THIS PEOPLE WITH YOUR MIGHT, HEAR THE NEWS, THEY WILL TELL IT TO THE OTHERS WHO LIVE IN THE LAND. "THEY HAVE HEARD THAT YOU, *ADONAI*, ARE WITH THIS PEOPLE, THAT YOU, *ADONAI*, WERE SEEN EYE-TO-EYE, YOUR CLOUD RESTING OVER THEM, WHEN YOU GO BEFORE THEM IN A PILLAR OF CLOUD BY DAY AND IN A PILLAR OF FIRE BY NIGHT. "IF THEN YOU KILL EVERY ONE OF THIS PEOPLE THE NATIONS WHO HAVE HEARD OF YOUR FAME WILL SAY, 'IT MUST BE BECAUSE *ADONAI* WAS POWERLESS TO BRING THAT PEOPLE INTO THE LAND WHICH GOD HAD PROMISED THEM. GOD KILLED THEM IN THE DESERT.' "THEREFORE, I PRAY, LET *ADONAI*'S POWER (TO FORGIVE) BE GREAT, AS YOU HAVE SAID, '*ADONAI*, SLOW TO ANGER AND WITH MUCH KINDNESS, FORGIVING SIN AND TRANSGRESSION, CLEARING AWAY AND NOT CLEARING AWAY ALL PUNISHMENT, BUT VISITING THE SINS OF THE PARENTS ON THE CHILDREN, UPON THE THIRD AND FOURTH GENERATIONS.' "FORGIVE, I PRAY, THE SINS OF THIS PEOPLE, FOR YOUR KINDNESS IS GREAT, JUST AS YOU HAVE FORGIVEN THIS PEOPLE EVER SINCE EGYPT." NUMBERS 14:13–19	

To find out the "short version" of God's response, check Numbers 14:20. For more detail on God's full reaction, read Numbers 14:20–35. Did Moses' conversation with God work?

What Is Shimon ben Elazar's Advice for the Adam and Eve Story?

Read through the story segment of Adam and Eve (Genesis 3:6–9), then check off the part of Shimon ben Elazar's advice that fits. Focus especially on the words in *italics*:

> THE WOMAN SAW THAT THE TREE WAS GOOD FOR EATING AND A DELIGHT FOR THE EYES, AND THE TREE WAS DESIRABLE FOR CREATING WISDOM. SHE TOOK FROM ITS FRUIT AND ATE IT AND GAVE IT ALSO TO HER HUSBAND, AND HE ATE. *THEN THEIR EYES OPENED AND THEY KNEW THAT THEY WERE NAKED.* THEY SEWED TOGETHER FIG LEAVES AND THEY MADE THEMSELVES A LOINCLOTH.

At this point, think about Adam and Eve. Were they angry? bereaved? about to make an oath? disgraced? Explain.

_____

_____

> THEY HEARD THE SOUND OF *ADONAI* MOVING ABOUT THE GARDEN IN THE BREEZY TIME OF DAY. *THE MAN AND WOMAN HID FROM BEFORE ADONAI-GOD*, AMONG THE TREES OF THE GARDEN.
> *ADONAI*-GOD CALLED TO THE MAN SAYING, "WHERE ARE YOU?"

Now think about God. Which part of Shimon ben Elazar's advice fits what God did in this situation?

- ☐ When your friend becomes angry, don't try to calm him.
- ☐ When he is recently bereaved, don't try to comfort him.
- ☐ When he is about to make an oath, don't ask him questions.
- ☐ Just after he has been disgraced, don't try to see him.

An Ending Thought from You

Making and keeping friends is not easy. Trying to figure out what our friends need from us at different times is hard work. Sometimes it is important for us to think about what we ourselves want in a specific situation. Take a moment and write what you would want your friends to do for you

- when you are angry. _____

_____

_____

- when someone you love has died. _____

_____

_____

- when you're about to make an important promise that may be hard to keep.

_____

_____

- when you've done something very embarrassing. _____

_____

_____

CONCERN FOR OTHERS

4:19

Shmuel HaKatan said,

שְׁמוּאֵל הַקָּטָן אוֹמֵר

"Do not rejoice when your enemy falls.

בִּנְפֹל אוֹיִבְךָ אַל תִּשְׂמָח

Do not let your heart be glad when another stumbles."

וּבִכָּשְׁלוֹ אַל יָגֵל לִבֶּךָ.

4:3

He [Ben Azzai] used to say,

הוּא הָיָה אוֹמֵר

"Treat no one lightly and think nothing is useless,

אַל תְּהִי בָז לְכָל אָדָם
וְאַל תְּהִי מַפְלִיג לְכָל דָּבָר

for everyone has his or her moment
and everything has its place."

שֶׁאֵין לְךָ אָדָם
שֶׁאֵין לוֹ שָׁעָה
וְאֵין לְךָ דָּבָר שֶׁאֵין לוֹ
מָקוֹם.

A Beginning Thought: Every person is created בְּצֶלֶם אֱלֹהִים, in the image of God.

בְּצֶלֶם אֱלֹהִים

In the image of God (*b'tzelem Elohim*).

In the Torah we read that "God created the human in God's image, in the image of God was [the human] created; male and female God created them." (Genesis 1:27) While our physical images are nothing like God (who has no physical image), our actions can imitate those of God. So while we praise God as "healer of the sick," we can do our part to help people get well. Even as we praise God for "raising up the fallen," we can use our strength to help others.

Spend a few moments thinking about some of the responsibilities we have in the world as a result of our creation in God's image. Create a "bubble diagram" of your thoughts.

Because we are created בְּצֶלֶם אֱלֹהִים, we have responsibilities to ...

Respecting Others

One of our responsibilities is to respect others, for like us, they are created in God's image. But that is often easier said than done because

- there are people we like.

- there are people we do not like.

- there are people we may not be friendly with, but we don't dislike them.

Shmuel HaKatan recognized human nature and therefore gave the following advice:

DO NOT REJOICE WHEN YOUR ENEMY FALLS.
DO NOT LET YOUR HEART BE GLAD WHEN ANOTHER STUMBLES.

1. With a partner, read the comic below.

2. Together, first figure out who might rejoice. Then, write a conversation of the boy telling one of his friends what happened. He should talk as if he has

studied Shmuel HaKatan's advice. Make sure that the friend asks at least two questions that the boy answers.

Boy: _____

His friend: _____

Boy: _____

His friend: _____

Boy: _____

His friend: _____

Boy: _____

Treat No One Lightly

In the late 1990s a new slang word appeared in the English language: "dis," short for "disrespect." It is used in such sentences as "Hey, don't dis me!" (don't show me disrespect) or "He dissed me" (he was disrespectful).

Approximately 2,000 years ago, Ben Azzai also spoke about dissing, but in his own language. He said:

> TREAT NO ONE LIGHTLY AND THINK NOTHING IS USELESS,
> FOR EVERYONE HAS HIS OR HER MOMENT AND EVERYTHING HAS ITS PLACE.

Here is a story about Rabbi Akiva and his wife. Read it to figure out
- who was treated lightly (in other words, dissed).
- whether each person treated lightly "had his or her moment" (a time of greatness).

> RABBI AKIVA WAS THE SHEPHERD OF BEN KALBA SABUA. WHEN BEN KALBA SABUA'S DAUGHTER SAW HOW PIOUS AND CAPABLE RABBI AKIVA WAS, SHE ASKED HIM, "IF I BECOME ENGAGED TO YOU, WOULD YOU GO TO THE HOUSE OF STUDY?"
> HE SAID, "YES."

SO SHE SECRETLY BECAME ENGAGED TO HIM AND SENT HIM OFF TO LEARN. WHEN HER FATHER HEARD WHAT HIS DAUGHTER DID, HE SENT HER FROM HIS HOUSE AND VOWED THAT SHE WOULD NOT INHERIT ANY OF HIS MONEY.

AKIVA WENT AND STUDIED FOR TWELVE YEARS IN THE HOUSE OF STUDY. WHEN HE RETURNED, HE BROUGHT 12,000 STUDENTS WITH HIM. HE HEARD AN OLD MAN SAY TO HIS [AKIVA'S] WIFE, "HOW LONG STILL WILL YOU LIVE LIFE AS IF YOU WERE A WIDOW?"

SHE ANSWERED, "IF AKIVA LISTENED TO ME, HE WOULD STAY AWAY ANOTHER TWELVE YEARS."

SO AKIVA THOUGHT THAT IF HE DID THIS IT WOULD BE WITH HER PERMISSION. HE RETURNED TO THE HOUSE OF STUDY ANOTHER TWELVE YEARS. WHEN HE CAME BACK, HE BROUGHT 24,000 OF HIS STUDENTS WITH HIM.

WHEN HIS WIFE HEARD HE WAS COMING, SHE WENT OUT TO MEET HIM. HER NEIGHBORS SAID TO HER, "BORROW SOME CLOTHES AND DRESS UP IN THEM." [SHE WAS VERY POOR AND DID NOT HAVE MONEY FOR GOOD CLOTHING.]

BUT SHE SAID TO THEM, "THE RIGHTEOUS MAN KNOWS THE SOUL OF THE BEAST." [PROVERBS 12:10, MEANING THAT AKIVA, AS A RIGHTEOUS MAN, WOULD KNOW HER, EVEN IF SHE WERE NOT DRESSED WELL.]

WHEN SHE CAME TO HIM, SHE FELL DOWN AND KISSED HIS FEET.

AKIVA'S STUDENTS STARTED TO PUSH HER AWAY BUT HE SAID, "LET HER BE. WHAT IS MINE AND WHAT IS YOURS … IS HERS."

WHEN HER FATHER HEARD THAT A LEARNED MAN HAD COME TO THE CITY HE SAID [NOT KNOWING IT WAS AKIVA], "I WILL GO TO HIM. MAYBE HE WILL FREE ME OF MY VOW."

BEN KALBA SABUA CAME TO AKIVA AND TOLD AKIVA WHY HE [BEN KALBA SABUA] HAD MADE THE VOW.

AKIVA ASKED, "IF YOU HAD KNOWN

THAT HE WAS A LEARNED MAN, WOULD YOU HAVE MADE THE VOW?"

BEN KALBA SABUA SAID, "IF HE HAD KNOWN ONLY ONE SECTION, OR ONE LAW, I WOULD NOT HAVE MADE THE VOW."

THEN AKIVA TOLD HIM WHO HE WAS. BEN KALBA SABUA THEN FELL DOWN AND KISSED AKIVA'S FEET, AND GAVE HIM HALF OF HIS POSSESSIONS.

B. TALMUD *K'TUBOT* 62B–63A

 Discuss the story and then complete the chart together.

Who was treated lightly?	What moment of greatness did this person have (if any)?

Do you agree or disagree with Ben Azzai's advice? Explain your answer.

Who Gets Dissed Today?

In 1999, two boys from a high school in Columbine, Colorado, went on a shooting rampage in their school, killing a dozen students [and a teacher] and terrorizing hundreds of others. It was later discovered that these boys had felt like outcasts; they felt they had been treated lightly by others in their school. "Their moment," unfortunately, was one that caused great sorrow in their community and around the world.

 Take some time to think about someone you know who might feel as though he or she is being treated lightly by others. Do not mention him or her by name, but describe specific ways that others treat them (write these in the circles). Then, think about ways you might help the situation (write these in the rectangles).

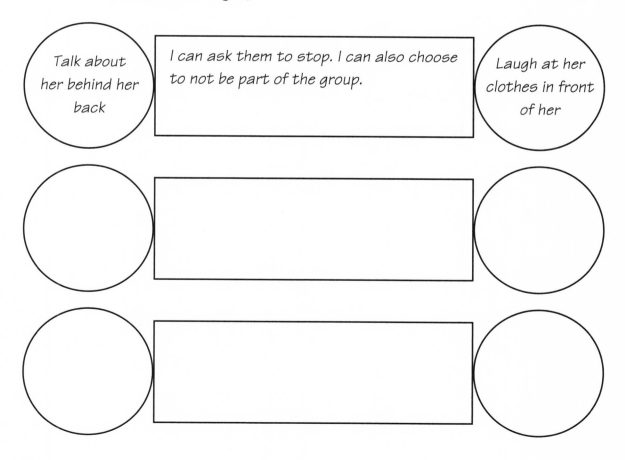

Talk about her behind her back

I can ask them to stop. I can also choose to not be part of the group.

Laugh at her clothes in front of her

An Ending Thought from You

In the Torah it says, "Love your neighbor as yourself; I am *Adonai*." (Leviticus 19:18) Why are these two thoughts written together in the same verse? Some say that our relationships with other humans are enhanced or made stronger by our relationship with God. Others say that we are to respect people different from ourselves because we are all created בְּצֶלֶם אֱלֹהִים, in the image of God.

- Think about the advice of Shmuel HaKatan and Ben Azzai. What responsibilities do they say you have to "love your neighbor"? _____

  _____

  _____

  _____

- What will you do differently in the next two days because you have studied their advice? _____

  _____

  _____

  _____

TREATING PEOPLE PROPERLY

Rabbi Yishmael would say,

רַבִּי יִשְׁמָעֵאל אוֹמֵר

"Be speedy to obey a superior.

הֱוֵי קַל לְרֹאשׁ

Be dignified before the young.

וְנוֹחַ לְתִשְׁחוֹרֶת

And cheerfully greet every person."

וֶהֱוֵי מְקַבֵּל אֶת כָּל הָאָדָם בְּשִׂמְחָה.

A Beginning Thought: Many people achieve success because they treat people properly.

One way to treat people properly begins with "reading faces" and responding in a way that is helpful to that person. To "read a face" we

- look at a person's facial expression.
- think about what emotion matches that expression.
- act appropriately.

With a partner, look at the faces below and fill in the chart:

	What emotion matches the expression?	**What would be a good way to act toward this person?**
		Calmly, or with some sympathy
	Embarrassment	

Another way to treat people properly is to consider their relationship to us. Rabbi Yishmael says:

BE SPEEDY TO OBEY A SUPERIOR.
BE DIGNIFIED BEFORE THE YOUNG.

In a group of two or three people do the following:

Chart what happens when you follow Rabbi Yishmael's advice, and when you choose to ignore it.

Give an example of a superior:	Give an example of someone younger:
_____	_____
(someone with more power than you, perhaps a teacher, parent, government official, or boss)	*(perhaps a brother or sister, a child in a younger class, a person you meet on the playground, or someone you babysit)*

⬇   ⬇

This person might ask us to do the following:

We might meet this young person in the following place:

_____   _____

⬇   ⬇

If we are quick to obey, this might happen:

If we are slow to obey, this might happen:

If we are dignified, this might happen:

If we are not dignified, this might happen:

_____   _____   _____   _____

_____   _____   _____   _____

⬇   ⬇   ⬇   ⬇

Our opinion of Rabbi Yishmael's advice is:

☐ Agree, because _____

_____

☐ Disagree, because _____

_____

Our opinion of Rabbi Yishmael's advice is:

☐ Agree, because _____

_____

☐ Disagree, because _____

_____

Different Translations

Sometimes, when translating from one language to another, experts have different opinions about the original meaning. The first line of this מִשְׁנָה can be translated in several different ways:

הֱוֵי קַל לְרֹאשׁ

BE SPEEDY TO OBEY A SUPERIOR.

KRAVITZ AND OLITZKY, EDITORS.
PIRKE AVOT: A MODERN COMMENTARY ON JEWISH ETHICS.

BE SUBMISSIVE TOWARD A GREAT PERSON.

HEREFORD, EDITOR.
ETHICS OF THE TALMUD: SAYINGS OF THE FATHERS.

BE SUBMISSIVE TO THE GOVERNMENT.

STERN, EDITOR.
PIRKE AVOT: WISDOM OF THE JEWISH SAGES.

In pairs, spend some time looking at some of the different translations by discussing these questions:

	Are there any words you need to look up in a dictionary? Write each new word and its meaning here.	Can you think of an example in real life when this statement is true? [Feel free to use one of the texts you studied earlier.]	Can you think of an example in real life when this statement is bad advice? [Feel free to use one of the texts you studied earlier.]
Be speedy to obey a superior.			
Be submissive toward a great person.			
Be submissive to the government.			

Joseph and Rabbi Yishmael's Advice

In the Torah, we learn that Joseph (once owner of a beautiful multicolored coat given to him by his father, Jacob) ends up in an Egyptian prison as a result of his brothers' anger and jealousy. As you know, he interprets two of Pharaoh's dreams and rises to power in time to save Egypt from a terrible famine. However, his brothers, starving in the land of Canaan, decide to travel to Egypt to buy food. The text, below, tells that when the brothers return to face Joseph a second time, they are asked to wait in his house.

> WHEN JOSEPH CAME TO THE HOUSE, THE BROTHERS CAME TO HIM WITH
> THE PRESENTS THAT WERE IN THEIR HANDS.... THEY BOWED TO HIM,
> TOWARD THE GROUND. HE ASKED HOW THEY WERE AND SAID, "IS YOUR OLD
> FATHER AT PEACE ... THE ONE YOU SPOKE OF. IS HE STILL ALIVE?"
> THEY SAID, "YOUR SERVANT, OUR FATHER, IS AT PEACE. HE STILL LIVES."
> THEY BOWED LOW.
>
> GENESIS 43:26–28

- Circle the translation that best fits the way the brothers treated Joseph:

  Be speedy to obey a superior.

  Be submissive toward a great person.

  Be submissive to the government.

- Why did you choose the translation you circled?

  _____

  _____

Cheerfully Greet Every Person

The Talmud (*B'rachot* 28a) tells us that 2,000 years ago, Rabbi Yochanan ben Zakkai always greeted others first, "even a non-Jew in the marketplace." The people of the tribes of Natal, in the northern part of South Africa, greet each other with *Sawu bona*, which means "I see you." One of the responses to *Sawu bona* is *Shikhona*, or "I am here." Think about this for a moment. How many of us walk by people without seeing them, without acknowledging them by saying "Hello"? *Sawu bona* has great power, for it reminds us that everyone deserves to be recognized.

The Hebrew greeting שָׁלוֹם also has power. When we use this word to greet someone, we understand that we are offering the gift of peace. Rabbi Natan, who lived after פִּרְקֵי אָבוֹת was completed as a book, commented on this third part of

our מִשְׁנָה. He noted that we need to think not only about our words (like "peace"),
but about our actions as well.

> IF WITH A GRUMPY FACE, YOU GIVE YOUR FELLOW PERSON ALL THE BEST
> GIFTS IN THE WORLD, JEWISH TRADITION SEES IT AS IF YOU HAD GIVEN THE
> PERSON NOTHING.
>
> BUT WHEN YOU GREET YOUR FELLOW PERSON WITH A CHEERFUL FACE,
> JEWISH TRADITION CREDITS YOU AS THOUGH YOU HAD GIVEN THE PERSON
> THE BEST GIFTS IN THE WORLD.
>
> *AVOT D'RABBI NATAN* 13, 29A

 Read the comic below and then answer the questions that follow.

1. Take a few moments to think about the "message" of the comic. What does it have
   to do with the words of the different rabbis?

   _____

   _____

   _____

2. What does it have to do with the *Sawu bona* greeting of the South African tribe?

   _____

   _____

   _____

Many People Achieve Success Because They Treat People Properly

There are many ways to be successful. Our מִשְׁנָה talks about three ways to treat people properly, but there are more ways. Here's a true story that illustrates this in today's world.

entrepreneur
A person who takes a risk starting up a new business.

ENTREPRENEUR TO SERVE TIME IN CONDEMNED RENTAL HOUSE

A NEWSPAPER STORY REPORTED THAT A 27-YEAR-OLD ENTREPRENEUR BOUGHT A CONDEMNED HOUSE [MEANING THAT IT WAS TOO DANGEROUS TO LIVE IN] AND THEN SOLD IT TO ANOTHER PERSON FOR 4 TIMES THE ORIGINAL PRICE—BUT WITHOUT FIXING THE HOUSE UP WITHIN A CERTAIN DEADLINE.

By many people's definition, this entrepreneur was successful because he earned lots of money on the sale of the house he bought. In other words, he was a financial success.

But the rabbis of פִּרְקֵי אָבוֹת would not have felt that the entrepreneur was successful because he did not treat people properly. In fact, the judge decided the entrepreneur's punishment was to live in the condemned house for 30 days.

Sit with two other people and make a list of people you know who are successful because they know how to treat people properly.

1. _____ is successful. This person treats people

   properly in the following way: _____

   _____.

2. _____ is successful. This person treats people

   properly in the following way: _____

   _____.

3. _____ is successful. This person treats people

   properly in the following way: _____

   _____.

4. _____ is successful. This person treats people

   properly in the following way: _____

   _____.

An Ending Thought from You

Fill in the blank for yourself!

I am successful because I treat people properly in the following ways:

_____

_____

_____

_____

JUMPING TO CONCLUSIONS

Hillel said …

הִלֵּל אוֹמֵר…

"Don't judge your fellow human being

וְאַל תָּדִין אֶת חֲבֵרְךָ

until you have reached that person's place."

עַד שֶׁתַּגִּיעַ לִמְקוֹמוֹ.

A Beginning Thought: It is very easy to jump to conclusions about others.

We sometimes think or say things about another person based on his or her appearance.

A person with thick glasses is sometimes judged to be a nerd.

A person with wrinkled skin is sometimes judged to be too old to understand "life in the modern world."

A person with torn clothes is sometimes judged to be too lazy to work.

We sometimes think or say things about another person before we really understand what is going on in his or her life.

An adult without a job is sometimes judged to be too lazy to work—but he may really have saved enough money to enjoy an early retirement.

A child who always daydreams in class is sometimes judged to be stupid—but she may really be working hard at home to take care of her siblings because her parents are going through a divorce.

Hillel tells us that it is important not to judge a person until you have "reached that person's place." There are many other ways we describe this in English:

- standing in a person's shoes…
- walking a mile in a person's moccasins…
- stepping into a person's place…
- standing in the place of…

These phrases are all metaphors for the same idea: **empathy**. Empathy is our ability to understand the feelings of another person. When we are able to reach a person's place, we can show empathy for a person.

These metaphors are important to keep in mind as you continue with this chapter.

Showing Empathy

 There are two stories about Moses' early life that give us clues about his relationships with others, and his empathy. The first one is from the Torah, and the second is a מִדְרָשׁ.

From the תּוֹרָה

In the Book of Exodus, we read of a time when Moses showed empathy to the Israelites while they were still slaves. As you read the verses with a partner, think about the impression someone might have about Moses from the incident:

> IN THOSE DAYS MOSES GREW UP AND WENT OUT TO HIS PEOPLE AND HE SAW THEIR SUFFERING. HE SAW AN EGYPTIAN MAN STRIKE A HEBREW MAN FROM AMONG HIS PEOPLE.
>
> MOSES TURNED THIS WAY AND THAT WAY AND SAW THAT THERE WAS NO PERSON [LOOKING] SO HE HIT THE EGYPTIAN [AND KILLED HIM] THEN HID HIM IN THE SAND.
>
> EXODUS 2:11–12

1. How did Moses show that he "stood in the place" of the Hebrew?

   _____

   _____

2. If you were hiding behind a rock and saw this, what might you think about Moses?

   _____

   _____

empathy

A person's ability to understand the feelings of someone else.

מִדְרָשׁ

A story that helps explain something unclear in the Bible. A *midrash* usually fills in a hole that the Bible leaves open. (The plural form is מִדְרָשִׁים [*midrashim*].)

3. What did the Hebrews think about his actions? Read the rest of the story, in Exodus 2:13–14, to find out.

_____

_____

From the מִדְרָשׁ

A מִדְרָשׁ is a story that "fills in the blanks" of a Torah story. One of the most famous מִדְרָשִׁים (midrashim; plural form of midrash) is of Abraham smashing the idols in his father's shop when he was a young boy. The Torah gives no details of Abraham's younger life that would help us understand why he came to believe in one God. So the rabbis filled in the gap with a מִדְרָשׁ in which he tells his father that the larger idols smashed the smaller idols.

 Here is a מִדְרָשׁ told of Moses. Read it and then complete the statements that follow.

WHILE MOSES WAS SHEPHERDING JETHRO'S SHEEP IN THE DESERT, A LAMB RAN AWAY FROM HIM. HE RAN AFTER HER UNTIL HE FOUND THE LAMB DRINKING AT A POOL OF WATER.

WHEN MOSES REACHED HER HE SAID, "I DID NOT KNOW THAT YOU RAN AWAY BECAUSE YOU WERE THIRSTY. YOU MUST BE TIRED." MOSES PLACED THE LAMB ON HIS SHOULDER AND BEGAN TO WALK.

SH'MOT RABBAH 2:2

1. Moses might have prejudged the lamb and thought that it ran away because

_____.

2. But, Moses put himself in the lamb's place and decided that the lamb ran away because

_____.

What is interesting about this מִדְרָשׁ is that God watches Moses and draws a conclusion about him from his actions. The last few lines of this מִדְרָשׁ are:

> ADONAI SAID, "YOU ARE COMPASSIONATE IN LEADING ANIMALS BELONGING TO PEOPLE. I SWEAR YOU WILL SIMILARLY LEAD MY FLOCK, THE PEOPLE OF ISRAEL."

Did Moses Fulfill God's Expectations? Did God Act with Compassion?

 From the מִדְרָשׁ about Moses and the lamb we learn that God expected Moses to show empathy for the Hebrews as he led them out of Egypt and into the desert. Did this really happen? And what about God? Did God show compassion to the Israelites in the desert? Was God able to "stand in their place" and empathize?

Below are references to three stories from the Torah about the Israelites in the desert. With two or three classmates, find each story in the Torah and then decide whether Moses or God did the better job of "standing in the place" of the Israelites (showing them empathy) as they ran into food problems in the desert.

Food problems Exodus 16:1–9	Water problems Exodus 17:1–7	More food problems Numbers 11:1–23
☐ God did the better job.	☐ God did the better job.	☐ God did the better job.
☐ Moses did the better job.	☐ Moses did the better job.	☐ Moses did the better job.
☐ They did an equal job.	☐ They did an equal job.	☐ They did an equal job.

"Reaching a Person's Place" ... with Classmates

Many people don't stop to think about how they judge people before they know them better. But we do it all the time. Working in a group of three or four students, see how you can use Hillel's advice when examining classroom situations.

Below are three different kinds of cards, each with different kinds of information:

- The *behavior* we see people do … or what we hear them say. These cards have a picture of a person on them.

- The *reason(s)* why people do or say those things. These cards have a picture of footprints on them, so you can stand in their place.

- The *actions* we can do to help those people. These cards have a helping hand on them.

There are also two blank cards for each category. They are for you to fill in with your group's ideas.

 With 2 or 3 other people, photocopy pages 104, 105 and 106, cut out the cards and match them up. Be sure to match each behavior card with one footprint card and one helping hand card.

There is no one right way to make matches! Your group just needs to be logical in connecting each of the pieces together. As long as you can explain to another group or to your teacher why you put the pieces together, your matches are just fine. Here's an example of a match:

Jay came to school in dirty clothes.

This was written on a Behavior card.

His mother just took a new job and was having trouble doing the laundry.

The group wrote this idea on a Footprint card.

Your friends decide not to call Jay names, like "Stinky."

This was written on a Helping Hand.

Hint: Begin by laying all the Person cards in a line. Then match the Footprint cards one at a time next to the Person cards. Finally, match the Helping Hand cards in the last row or column.

Matt had a very hard time learning Hebrew. He rarely read a line out loud correctly.	Mark was nine years old. He slammed his textbook to the floor a lot in class.	
Yoni always played with Shira on the playground. He never played with anyone else.		Eli always seemed to speak in a loud voice. He had a hard time speaking softly.

His parents shouted at each other at home a lot. He was worried that they might get a divorce.	He was born with a hearing problem.	He had just moved from another city and was having a hard time making friends.
	His brother will be celebrating his bar mitzvah in a few weeks. He is getting a lot of attention at home.	

	Invite him over to your house to play.	
Speak in a soft, kind voice to him.	Be very patient with him in class. Try to ignore the problem.	Offer to help him with his classwork.

An Ending Thought from You

It's not easy learning to empathize with other people. But when we put ourselves in another person's place, we can often figure out what that person needs from us. Sometimes we can do this by just watching and listening carefully. But sometimes we need to ask directly, "What's going on? How may I be helpful to you?"

 • Whom do you know that you might have judged wrongly?

_____

• How will you "stand in his or her place"? _____

_____

BE A MENSCH!

He [Hillel] said…

"In a place where there are no human beings,
try to be one."

הוּא הָיָה אוֹמֵר...

וּבְמָקוֹם שֶׁאֵין אֲנָשִׁים

הִשְׁתַּדֵּל לִהְיוֹת אִישׁ.

A Beginning Thought: One of the highest praises we can give someone is the label "mensch."

"Mensch" is a Yiddish word that represents one of the highest ideals a person can reach.

A mensch is a decent, upright, human being.

A mensch is someone who thinks and acts from the heart to help others.

A mensch takes action when others might not lift a finger.

A mensch is a person worthy to be our friend.

To be called a mensch is great praise, indeed.

 With a partner, look carefully at the definition of a mensch. Whom do you know who might be called a mensch? It could be a person in your school, a sports or political figure, or someone you've read about in the news.

1. Who is the person you chose? _____

2. Why is she or he a mensch? _____

_____

_____

_____

Who Is a Mensch?

The Talmud, a book of Jewish law compiled more than 1,500 years ago, has some wonderful stories demonstrating *menschlekeit* behavior (that means acting like a mensch). Below are two such stories. Divide into three groups, and:

1. Read one of the stories below, as assigned by your teacher.
2. Discuss the story with your partners, focusing on the *menschlekeit* behavior.
   • In your book, circle the name of the person (or people) acting like a mensch.
   • List several reasons why the behavior is *menschlekeit*.
3. Prepare a skit of your story for the rest of the class. Do not specifically identify the *menschlekeit* behavior. When you are done, ask the class to identify who was the mensch.

Story A

RABBI GIDDAL WAS NEGOTIATING FOR A CERTAIN FIELD, AND RABBI ABBAH WENT AHEAD AND BOUGHT IT. RABBI GIDDAL THEN COMPLAINED TO RABBI ZE'EIRA, WHO IN TURN TOOK THE CASE TO RABBI YITZCHAK THE BLACKSMITH.

RABBI YITZCHAK SAID, "WAIT UNTIL RABBI ABBAH COMES TO JERUSALEM FOR THE NEXT FESTIVAL." [HE LIVED SOMEWHERE ELSE, BUT VISITED JERUSALEM FOR EACH OF THE THREE PILGRIMAGE FESTIVALS.]

WHEN HE CAME, RABBI YITZCHAK SAID TO HIM, "IF A POOR MAN IS EXAMINING A CAKE AND ANOTHER COMES AND TAKES IT AWAY FROM HIM, WHAT THEN?"

RABBI ABBAH SAID, "THEN HE IS CALLED WICKED."

RABBI YITZCHAK ASKED [REFERRING TO THE FIELD], "AND YOU, SIR, WHY DID YOU ACT AS YOU DID?"

RABBI ABBAH SAID, "I DID NOT KNOW HE WAS NEGOTIATING FOR IT."

RABBI YITZCHAK SAID, "THEN LET HIM HAVE IT NOW."

RABBI ABBAH SAID, "I WON'T SELL IT TO HIM BECAUSE IT IS THE FIRST FIELD I EVER BOUGHT, AND IT IS NOT A GOOD OMEN TO SELL IT. BUT IF HE WANTS IT AS A GIFT, HE CAN HAVE IT."

RABBI GIDDAL WAS TOO PROUD TO ACCEPT IT AS A GIFT, QUOTING THE BIBLICAL VERSE "HE THAT HATES GIFTS SHALL LIVE." AND RABBI ABBAH WOULD NOT TAKE POSSESSION OF IT NOW THAT HE KNEW RABBI GIDDAL HAD BEEN NEGOTIATING FOR IT. SO NEITHER TOOK THE LAND. IT BECAME KNOWN AS THE RABBIS' FIELD AND WAS USED AS A PLACE FOR STUDENTS TO GATHER.

B. TALMUD *KIDDUSHIN* 59A

Story B

IT HAPPENED THAT RABBI JUDAH HANASI ENTERED HIS LECTURE ROOM AND SMELLED GARLIC. HE SAID, "LET THE ONE WHO HAS EATEN GARLIC LEAVE THE ROOM."

THEN RABBI CHIYYA STOOD UP AND WENT OUT. THEN ALL THE STUDENTS GOT UP AND WENT OUT.

THE NEXT MORNING, RABBI SIMEON, THE SON OF JUDAH HANASI, WENT TO RABBI CHIYYA AND ASKED, "WERE YOU THE ONE WHO HAD BEEN EATING GARLIC?"

RABBI CHIYYA ANSWERED, "OF COURSE NOT, BUT BY OUR LEAVING, WE KEPT THE ONE RESPONSIBLE FROM BEING HUMILIATED."

B. TALMUD *SANHEDRIN* 11A

Following Hillel's Advice

What does it mean to "try to be a human being" in a place where there are none? It means recognizing that injustice is being done and that different action must be taken!

 With a partner, look at each of the situations listed on the next page. Then fill in the side of the chart that is open. Feel free to be creative in your stories. The first one has been done for you.

In a place where there are no human beings…	…try to be one
When Jonah made mistakes reading aloud in his social studies class, many of the students snickered.	*Bill sat as quietly as he could, listening respectfully to Jonah read.*
	Sarah offered Carly some of her lunch.
Most of the people passing the homeless man averted their eyes and walked as far away from him as possible.	
A group of students walked away from their picnic lunch and started to play baseball together. At the end of the afternoon, they left their mess and went home.	
	Jamie knew that she'd miss her favorite TV show, but she also knew that Yael, her best friend, really needed help. So she turned off the TV and said, "Yes, I will."
	Paul put his hand on his sister's shoulder and sat beside her. He said, "Tell me more."

An Ending Thought from You

One of the greatest things we can say about someone is that she or he is a mensch. There are people who behave like a mensch all the time. And there are lots of people who perform acts of *menschlekeit* behavior—they do things that are "mensch-like."

When have you been *menschlekeit*? Make a list of three things you have done:

1. _____

2. _____

3. _____

Think about your coming week. When might you be able to do something *menschlekeit* for someone else?

_____

_____

Unit Wrap-Up

פִּרְקֵי אָבוֹת on Relationships

And if I am for myself alone, then what am I?

When a person no longer thinks "for myself alone," then he or she is concerned about relationships with others. And so this unit focused on what פִּרְקֵי אָבוֹת had to say about relationships. As humans created בְּצֶלֶם אֱלֹהִים (in the image of God) we have a special responsibility to take care of ourselves and to help others. We learned that one of the highest ideals of Jewish life is to behave as a mensch.

There's a Hebrew phrase, דֶּרֶךְ אֶרֶץ, that means "appropriate behavior." When we treat others well, when we do not act "for myself alone," then we are behaving with דֶּרֶךְ אֶרֶץ.

In what ways can you behave with דֶּרֶךְ אֶרֶץ in the future?
    To your family?
    To your friends?
    To your teachers?

How will you be a mensch this week?

- What is the most important thing you learned from this unit? _____
  _____
  _____

- Why is it important to you? _____
  _____
  _____

UNIT III

IF NOT NOW, WHEN?

FOUR KINDS OF PEOPLE

There are four kinds of people who would give צְדָקָה.

אַרְבַּע מִדּוֹת בְּנוֹתְנֵי צְדָקָה.

One who wishes to give
but [believes] that others should not.
That one's eye is evil to those others.

הָרוֹצֶה שֶׁיִּתֵּן
וְלֹא יִתְּנוּ אֲחֵרִים
עֵינוֹ רָעָה בְּשֶׁל אֲחֵרִים.

One who [wishes that] others give and
that he should not.
His eye is evil toward himself.

יִתְּנוּ אֲחֵרִים
וְהוּא לֹא יִתֵּן
עֵינוֹ רָעָה בְּשֶׁלּוֹ.

One who [wishes that] he should give
and so should others.
That is the best way.

יִתֵּן
וְיִתְּנוּ אֲחֵרִים
חָסִיד.

[The] one [who believes that he] should
   not give,
nor should others,
that is the worst way.

לֹא יִתֵּן
וְלֹא יִתְּנוּ אֲחֵרִים
רָשָׁע.

A Beginning Thought: One's words and actions can influence other people.

Have you ever stopped to think about the power of commercials and advertisements? The people who create them want to persuade you to purchase something—and quite often they succeed! Maybe an advertisement for shoes influences you to purchase a specific name brand. Or, maybe the food in a commercial seems so mouthwatering that you beg your family to go to a certain restaurant next time you eat out.

 People can influence you as well. In what ways have these people influenced you to do something, believe something, or try something new?

- A parent_____

- A teacher _____

- A friend _____

- A character in a movie or a book _____

_____

> **צְדָקָה**
>
> (Tzedakah); an obligation to give money to others to help them fulfill their basic needs.

This מִשְׁנָה describes four kinds of people who want to influence the giving habits of others.

Giving to Others

There are many ways we can give to others. This specific מִשְׁנָה is about the giving of צְדָקָה—our obligation to help others with money. In English we call this "charity," but the Hebrew focuses more on our sense of responsibility; the root is צ-ד-ק, meaning "justice" or "righteousness."

Work with a partner to read through and "diagram" this מִשְׁנָה. What is it telling us?

What the person wants for him or herself	What the person wants for other people	How the מִשְׁנָה labels this person
I should give	Others should not give	"evil to others"

Giving in Real Life

 It seems strange that people might ask others to give צְדָקָה but *not* do so themselves. Yet, it happens. To find out how, work with a partner to match each thought from פִּרְקֵי אָבוֹת with the appropriate example.

1. One who wishes to give but believes that others should not. ____

2. One who wishes that others give and that he should not. ____

3. One who wishes that he should give and so should others. ____

4. One who believes that he should not give, nor should others. ____

A. Ben takes out money to buy a raffle ticket for a friend's school and tells those standing with him that it's for a good cause.

B. Hannah's mom tears up the donation letter that came in the mail from a well-known center for the homeless. The mom wants no one in the family to make a donation to them because she believes that homeless people are too lazy to work.

C. Megan gives five dollars to a homeless man and tells her friends who are with her not to take out their wallets because she "took care of him."

D. Michael volunteers to be the class chairperson for the annual Tu BiSh'vat tree campaign. He himself buys no trees.

What examples can you think of from real life? Pick two of the four types of people and write your own scenarios:

What פִּרְקֵי אָבוֹת says	A real-life example

Thinking about Two Other Rabbis

 Work in a group of three or four students to figure out what kind of people Rabbi Yannai and Rabbi Tarfon are, based on the מִשְׁנָה of giving צְדָקָה.

Story A

RABBI YANNAI SAW SOMEONE GIVING MONEY TO A POOR PERSON PUBLICLY. HE SAID TO THE MAN, "BETTER NOT TO GIVE IT, THAN TO GIVE IT AND TO MAKE THE POOR PERSON ASHAMED."

B. TALMUD *CHAGIGAH* 5A

1. In your own words, what did Rabbi Yannai say to the other man?

_____

_____

2. Did Rabbi Yannai himself
   ☐ give? ☐ not give? ☐ we don't know

3. Did Rabbi Yannai try to influence the man
   ☐ to give? ☐ not to give? ☐ we don't know

4. Why does this story of Rabbi Yannai not exactly fit the four types of people described in the מִשְׁנָה?

   _____

   _____

Story B

> RABBI TARFON WAS TEACHING HIS STUDENTS WHEN A [VERY POOR ORPHANED] BRIDE PASSED BY. HE ORDERED THAT SHE SHOULD BE BROUGHT INTO HIS HOUSE. THEN HE TOLD HIS WIFE AND MOTHER TO BATHE HER, PUT PERFUMES ON HER, DRESS HER UP, AND DANCE WITH HER UNTIL SHE WENT TO HER HUSBAND'S HOUSE.
>
> *AVOT D'RABBI NATAN, 41, 67A*

1. In your own words, what did Rabbi Tarfon tell the others? _____

   _____

2. Did Rabbi Tarfon himself
   ☐ give? ☐ not give? ☐ we don't know

3. Did Rabbi Tarfon try to influence his wife and mother
   ☐ to give? ☐ not to give? ☐ we don't know

4. According to our מִשְׁנָה, what type of person would Rabbi Tarfon be?

   _____

   _____

Wanting Others to Do What *We* Want

In this מִשְׁנָה, we learn about four different types of people who want others to behave in certain ways. But this raises other questions about fairness.

 Spend some time talking with two or three other students to answer these two questions:

1. Is it reasonable to wish that other people behave the way *we* want them to? Explain your answer.

_____

_____

_____

_____

_____

2. Does it make a difference if what we want them to do is for a **reputable** cause? Explain your answer.

_____

_____

_____

_____

_____

_____

reputable
Something (or someone) with a good reputation; known to be honest or trustworthy.

An Ending Thought from You

In Unit III of the book, each מִשְׁנָה we will study has something to do about helping others. The one in this chapter is not only about helping others by *giving* צְדָקָה, but also about *influencing* others to give—or not to give. Take some time and think about how *you* wish to influence others.

• What do you wish people would do to help others? _____

_____

_____

_____

_____

• What can *you* do to influence people to do what you wish? _____

_____

_____

_____

_____

BE LIKE AARON

Hillel said,

"Be one of Aaron's students,

　loving peace and pursuing it,

　loving people

　and bringing them to the Torah."

הִלֵּל אוֹמֵר

הֱוֵי מִתַּלְמִידָיו שֶׁל אַהֲרֹן

אוֹהֵב שָׁלוֹם וְרוֹדֵף שָׁלוֹם

אוֹהֵב אֶת הַבְּרִיּוֹת

וּמְקָרְבָן לַתּוֹרָה.

role model
Someone who influences our lives. This person models actions and ideas that we find important enough to do ourselves.

A Beginning Thought: The lives of great people can influence our own actions.

In the last chapter, we saw how the strong feelings of one person can influence the lives of others. For example, your father may influence your decision on giving צְדָקָה by telling you his thoughts about a specific organization. Or, a friend may tell you about a rally to protest against a certain cause and even offer to have her parents drive you there. In that chapter, *others* wanted to influence us!

In this chapter, we will think about finding people *we* want to influence us. We will explore what it means to choose a personal **role model** to influence our lives.

 Find three people (either adults or people your age) and ask them the questions below. Use that information to complete the chart that follows. Be prepared to share your answers with your classmates.

1. Do you have a role model, or someone who influences your life? Who is it?
2. How does this person influence you?

Person interviewed	Role model	Influence of role model

Be One of Aaron's Students

In school, we are assigned to be the student of specific teachers. We may be math students of Mrs. Schwartz's and language arts students of Mr. Birmingham's.

 Which teachers have you really enjoyed? As their student, what did you learn from each?

- I enjoyed being the student of _____.

  I learned _____.

- I enjoyed being the student of _____.

  I learned _____.

- I enjoyed being the student of _____.

  I learned _____.

Hillel, a rabbi who lived more than 2,000 years ago, tells us that one of his favorite teachers was Moses' brother, Aaron, who lived more than 3,000 years ago. Hillel tells us what to learn from Aaron, as if we ourselves were his [Aaron's] student:

LOVE PEACE (אוֹהֵב שָׁלוֹם)   AND   PURSUE PEACE (רוֹדֵף שָׁלוֹם)

 Work with a partner to answer the questions written below the doves:

How might someone show that he or she loves peace?

How might someone show that he or she pursues peace?

What are the differences between loving peace and pursuing peace?

Loving and Pursuing Peace

Aaron was passionate about peace—he loved it and pursued it. A book called *Avot D'Rabbi Natan* tells several מִדְרָשִׁים that explain (1) why Hillel suggests we should be one of Aaron's students *and* (2) the meaning of a verse from the Book of Numbers that says, "All the house of Israel wept [for Aaron when he died]."

One מִדְרָשׁ states,

> IF TWO PEOPLE ARGUED, AARON WOULD SIT BY ONE OF THEM AND SAY, "SEE WHAT YOUR FRIEND SAYS. YOUR FRIEND IS TEARING HIS HEART AND RIPPING HIS CLOTHING SAYING, 'WOE IS ME! HOW SHALL I LOOK AT MY NEIGHBOR? I AM ASHAMED, FOR I HAVE SINNED AGAINST HIM.'"
>
> AARON SAT WITH THE FIRST PERSON UNTIL HE WAS NO LONGER ANGRY.
>
> THEN AARON WENT AND DID THE SAME THING TO THE OTHER PERSON.
>
> WHEN THE TWO PEOPLE WHO HAD ARGUED FINALLY GOT TOGETHER, THEY HUGGED AND KISSED EACH OTHER.
>
> *AVOT D'RABBI NATAN* (VERS. 1), 12, 24B–25A

Another מִדְרָשׁ tells the same general story, but with a husband and wife as the main characters. It says that if a man argued with his wife, then Aaron would spend time going from husband to wife repeatedly, helping them work things out until all was well again between the two. But this story ends in a special way:

> AFTER A WHILE, THE WIFE WOULD HAVE A BABY AND SHE WOULD SAY, "IT IS BECAUSE OF AARON THAT THIS SON HAS BEEN GIVEN TO ME." [SHE WOULD NAME THE BOY AARON.]
>
> SOME SAY THAT THERE WERE MORE THAN 3,000 ISRAELITES CALLED AARON.
>
> AND SO, WHEN AARON DIED, IT SAYS THAT "ALL THE CONGREGATION WEPT FOR HIM."
>
> *AVOT D'RABBI NATAN* (VERS. 2), 25, 25B

1. How do we know that Aaron loved peace and pursued peace?

    _____

    _____

    _____

2. Why did all of the Israelites cry when Aaron died?

    _____

    _____

    _____

Loving and Pursuing Other Important Issues

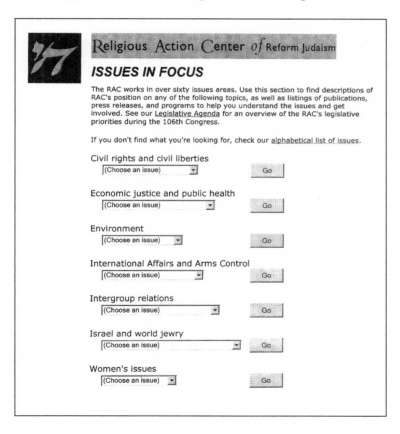

Some people pick Aaron as a role model because of his passion for pursuing peace. But there are other important causes and issues one may feel strongly about. The UAHC's Religious Action Center (RAC) passionately pursues a large number of issues nationally and internationally. The Religious Action Center's home page may be found at www.rac.org.

With two or four other students, examine the "Issues in Focus" page from the RAC's website reprinted on page 127 or check out the website itself. Fill in the chart below using the information you discover and your own thinking:

A person who is passionate about this issue...	...might be a role model and influence others by pursuing these actions.

Be a Student of...

Hillel tells us that we should make ourselves students of Aaron, the brother of Moses. Hillel even gives us samples of what Aaron "teaches."

Think of someone who has been your teacher. (He or she can be a parent, a friend, a rabbi, teacher, or someone whom you have never met but have read about or seen on television.) Create an advertisement about that person for a magazine, using a style that emulates (follows the model of) Hillel's quote in פִּרְקֵי אָבוֹת. It could follow this pattern:

BE ONE OF _____ 'S STUDENTS,

LOVING _____ AND _____ IT.

Illustrate your ad so that it catches the eye of someone your age. Use the space below.

An Ending Thought from You

If Hillel spoke about you, what would he say? Fill in the blanks.

Be one of the students of _____.

Love _____ and pursue _____.

WISDOM VS. DEEDS

3:9

Rabbi Chanina ben Dosa said…

רַבִּי חֲנִינָא בֶּן דּוֹסָא אוֹמֵר…

"One whose deeds are greater than one's wisdom, one's wisdom will last.

כֹּל שֶׁמַּעֲשָׂיו מְרֻבִּין מֵחָכְמָתוֹ חָכְמָתוֹ מִתְקַיֶּמֶת.

One whose wisdom is greater than one's deeds, one's wisdom will not last."

וְכֹל שֶׁחָכְמָתוֹ מְרֻבָּה מִמַּעֲשָׂיו אֵין חָכְמָתוֹ מִתְקַיֶּמֶת.

3:17

Rabbi Elazar ben Azaryah said…

רַבִּי אֶלְעָזָר בֶּן עֲזַרְיָה אוֹמֵר…

"When our wisdom
is greater than our deeds,
what are we like?

כֹּל שֶׁחָכְמָתוֹ
מְרֻבָּה מִמַּעֲשָׂיו
לְמָה הוּא דוֹמֶה?

Like a tree whose branches are many
but whose roots are few
so that when the wind comes,
it will uproot it and overturn it….

לְאִילָן שֶׁעֲנָפָיו מְרֻבִּין
וְשָׁרָשָׁיו מוּעָטִין
וְהָרוּחַ בָּאָה וְעוֹקַרְתּוֹ
וְהוֹפַכְתּוֹ עַל פָּנָיו….

But when our deeds
are greater than our wisdom,
what are we like?

אֲבָל כֹּל שֶׁמַּעֲשָׂיו
מְרֻבִּין מֵחָכְמָתוֹ
לְמָה הוּא דוֹמֶה?

Like a tree whose branches are few,
but whose roots are many,
so that even if all the winds of the
world were to come and blow on it,
it would not move from its place."

לְאִילָן שֶׁעֲנָפָיו מוּעָטִין
וְשָׁרָשָׁיו מְרֻבִּין
שֶׁאֲפִלּוּ כָּל הָרוּחוֹת שֶׁבָּעוֹלָם
בָּאוֹת וְנוֹשְׁבוֹת בּוֹ
אֵין מְזִיזִין אוֹתוֹ מִמְּקוֹמוֹ....

A Beginning Thought: Balance in life is important.

Life is filled with a great many choices. A student who finds herself running from
school to ballet, to band practice, to play rehearsals, to an aerobics class, to religious
school, may need to set some priorities. If "overprogrammed," she might have to
figure out which activities help her achieve her life goals, and then eliminate one or
two that are the least important.

Are You in Balance?

Being "in balance" does not mean that everything in your
life must be equal. A balanced diet *does not* mean

- 7 fruit and vegetable servings per day.
- 7 bread servings per day.
- 7 meat servings per day.
- 7 fat servings per day.

A balanced diet *does* mean that you have the right amount of each kind of food that
creates a healthy you.

A life in balance means that you have found a way to do the things that
- you want to do (like joining the school band).
- help you achieve your life goals (like performing in a school play if your goal is to be an actor).
- educate you (like learning Hebrew or studying ballet).
- keep you healthy (like visiting the dentist).
- do not overwhelm your time (like being able to do your homework *and* go to the mall with your friends).
- overall, make you feel like you have a fun and happy life.

 Below, make a list of the various things you do outside of regular school hours. You might want to turn the page sideways to write.

Sunday	Monday	Tuesday	Wednesday	Thursday	Friday	Saturday

Review the chart you just completed and answer the following questions.

1. How would you describe your time during the week?

    ☐ Not enough time to do what I want and need to do
    ☐ Just the right amount of time for everything
    ☐ Too much time with nothing to do

2. Do you feel that your life is in balance? _____

    Explain why or why not. _____

    _____

    _____

Balancing Wisdom with Deeds, Part I

The rabbis of פִּרְקֵי אָבוֹת talk about two things we need for balance in our lives:

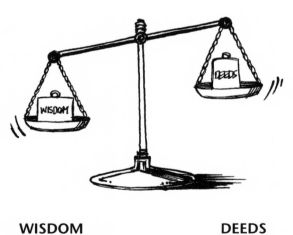

WISDOM	DEEDS
(or learning)	(or doing)

Work with one or two other people. First, read the words of Rabbi Chanina ben Dosa:

ONE WHOSE DEEDS ARE GREATER THAN ONE'S WISDOM, ONE'S WISDOM WILL LAST.

ONE WHOSE WISDOM IS GREATER THAN ONE'S DEEDS, ONE'S WISDOM WILL NOT LAST.

Now read the descriptions that follow. According to Rabbi Chanina ben Dosa, will these people's wisdom (or learning) last? Circle Yes or No.

1. Alison reads OK (not great, but OK) in Hebrew class, but she does *not* practice reading for ten minutes each night, as her teacher has asked.

   Yes   No

2. Max had a really hard time remembering the correct tune for the Torah blessings, but every night he sang along with the tape his cantor made.

   Yes   No

3. Elana's parents decided to learn more about the holiday of Shavuot. They began by buying a book on Jewish holidays, and each read the chapter on Shavuot. They made a commitment to go to services this year and to choose one of the holiday's mitzvot to follow.

   Yes   No

4. Mark's teacher required each of the students to do ten hours of community service (for example, serving dinner at a soup kitchen, sorting donated clothing, or tutoring a younger student). She *also* asked the students to make a poster showing why Judaism says we should get involved in helping. Mark loved volunteering for a local veterinarian and did forty hours of work, but decided to "forget" to research what Judaism says about helping animals.

   Yes   No

5. Jacob asked each of his aunts and uncles to buy tickets for his synagogue's raffle. But when they asked him what the money was going to be used for, he did not know what to say because he had not read the sheet that came with the tickets.

   Yes   No

Balancing Wisdom with Deeds, Part II

 Using a tree as his metaphor, Rabbi Elazar ben Azaryah explains how to balance wisdom and deeds in our lives. With the same group you have been working with, read through the quote of Rabbi Elazar ben Azaryah and then create a poster illustrating his thoughts. Use the space below to sketch your ideas:

Sketch 1

WHEN OUR WISDOM IS GREATER THAN OUR DEEDS, WHAT ARE WE LIKE? LIKE A TREE WHOSE BRANCHES ARE MANY BUT WHOSE ROOTS ARE FEW, SO THAT WHEN THE WIND COMES, IT WILL UPROOT IT AND OVERTURN IT.

Sketch 2

WHEN OUR DEEDS ARE GREATER THAN OUR WISDOM, WHAT ARE WE LIKE? LIKE A TREE WHOSE BRANCHES ARE FEW, BUT WHOSE ROOTS ARE MANY, SO THAT EVEN IF ALL THE WINDS OF THE WORLD WERE TO COME AND BLOW ON IT, IT WOULD NOT MOVE FROM ITS PLACE.

Will Rabbi Chiyya's Wisdom Last?

 Read this story about Rabbi Chiyya and decide
- whether his wisdom will last (according to Rabbi Chanina ben Dosa).
- which tree is a metaphor for his life (according to Rabbi Elazar ben Azaryah).

Rabbi Chiyya said,

TO MAKE SURE THAT תּוֹרָה WOULD NOT BE FORGOTTEN IN ISRAEL, WHAT DID I DO? I SOWED FLAX, AND FROM THE FLAX CORDS I MADE NETS.

WITH THE NETS I TRAPPED DEER, GAVE THEIR MEAT TO ORPHANS TO EAT, AND FROM THEIR SKINS I PREPARED SCROLLS.

ON THE SCROLLS I WROTE THE תּוֹרָה. THEN I WENT TO A TOWN THAT HAD NO TEACHERS AND TAUGHT THE FIVE BOOKS [OF MOSES] TO FIVE CHILDREN, AND THE SIX ORDERS OF THE MISHNAH TO SIX CHILDREN.

I TOLD THEM, "UNTIL I RETURN, TEACH EACH OTHER THE תּוֹרָה AND THE MISHNAH."

AND THAT IS HOW I KEPT THE תּוֹרָה FROM BEING FORGOTTEN IN ISRAEL.

B. TALMUD *BAVA M'TZIA* 85B

1. Will Rabbi Chiyya's wisdom last? _____

   Explain. _____

2. What kind of tree would illustrate Rabbi Chiyya's actions? _____

   _____

An Ending Thought from You

 • Based on your current "balance of life," will your wisdom last?_____

   Explain. _____

   _____

• What kind of tree best illustrates your balance of wisdom and actions?_____

   Why? _____

   _____

THE WORLD STANDS ON THREE THINGS

1:2

He [Rabbi Shimon HaTzadik] used to say,
   "The world stands on three things:

הוּא הָיָה אוֹמֵר
עַל שְׁלֹשָׁה דְבָרִים הָעוֹלָם עוֹמֵד

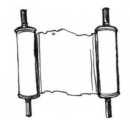

on the Torah,

עַל הַתּוֹרָה

on worship,

וְעַל הָעֲבוֹדָה

and on acts of loving-kindness."

וְעַל גְּמִילוּת חֲסָדִים.

1:18

Rabban Shimon ben Gamliel said,
  "The world stands on three things:

רַבָּן שִׁמְעוֹן בֶּן גַּמְלִיאֵל אוֹמֵר
עַל שְׁלשָׁה דְבָרִים הָעוֹלָם קַיָּם

on truth,

עַל הָאֱמֶת

on justice,

וְעַל הַדִּין

and on peace."

וְעַל הַשָּׁלוֹם.

A Beginning Thought: Jewish tradition respects and allows different opinions.

But there are basic ideas about Judaism that are the foundation of our religion and that are respected by everyone.

There's an old joke that Jews tell about ourselves: If two Jews are having a discussion, a person listening carefully to their ideas can often hear at least three different opinions. Or you might have heard the expression, "Two Jews, three opinions." In the last lesson, we saw that Rabbi Chanina ben Dosa and Rabbi Elazar ben Azaryah each had something to say about wisdom and taking action—but they had their own way of talking about the ideas. In this lesson, we have two rabbis each offering an opinion about the three most important things in the world!

What's Different?

 Work with a partner.

- First take a look at the words of Rabbi Shimon HaTzadik on page 139 and Rabban Shimon ben Gamliel on page 140.
- Then, examine the illustrations for Rabbi Shimon HaTzadik's idea.

1. Place a check next to the name of the rabbi whose words you think would be harder to illustrate.
   ☐ Rabbi Shimon HaTzadik (Torah, worship, and acts of loving-kindness)
   ☐ Rabban Shimon ben Gamliel (truth, justice, and peace)

2. Now go back and create your own illustrations for Rabban Shimon ben Gamliel.

What's the Same?

While "two Jews, three opinions" has some truth, the key ideas about Judaism are always the same. For example, while Jews talk about God in different ways, the key idea we all believe in is that there is one God.

Our two rabbis, Shimon HaTzadik and Shimon ben Gamliel, both say the world is based on three different things. But they have some key ideas that are similar.

With three other people, match up an idea of Shimon HaTzadik with an idea of Shimon ben Gamliel. Which seem to go together?

• _____ is similar to _____

  because _____

  _____.

• _____ is similar to _____

  because _____

  _____.

• _____ is similar to _____

  because _____

  _____.

Focus on Rabbi Shimon HaTzadik's Top Three

Here's a chance to test your detective skills. Your job is to find out what Shimon HaTzadik meant when he said that the world stands on Torah, worship, and acts of loving-kindness.

Divide into three groups, with each group working on *one* of Shimon's top three. You will share your detective work when done.

Group 1: The World Stands on Torah   עַל הַתּוֹרָה

Use these quotes from the Torah to help you figure out why Shimon HaTzadik believes that Torah is one of the three things on which the world stands. Write your ideas in the chart.

DO NOT STEAL.

EXODUS 20:13

WHEN YOU HARVEST YOUR LAND'S HARVEST, DO NOT HARVEST ALL THE WAY TO THE EDGES OF THE FIELD, OR PICK UP THE PARTS OF YOUR HARVEST THAT FELL. YOU SHALL NOT PICK YOUR VINEYARD BARE OR HARVEST YOUR VINEYARD'S FALLEN FRUIT. YOU SHALL LEAVE THEM FOR THE POOR AND THE STRANGER. I AM *ADONAI* YOUR GOD.

LEVITICUS 19:9–10

HEAR, O ISRAEL, *ADONAI* IS OUR GOD, *ADONAI* IS ONE.

DEUTERONOMY 6:4

In each of the squares, below, write down *one* thought from the Torah that you think is important to the world.	Write down *why* you think each thought from the Torah is important to the world.	Give some *examples of what people would need to do* to make that thought from the Torah happen in today's world.

Group 2: The World Stands on Worship

עַל הָעֲבוֹדָה

More than 2,000 years ago, even before the time of Shimon HaTzadik, Jews prayed by sacrificing animals to God, saying prayers, and singing songs from the Bible. Today we use words of prayer to communicate with God. Use these prayers from the prayer book to help you figure out why Shimon HaTzadik believes that worship is one of the three things on which the world stands. Write your ideas in the chart.

For Health

Heal us, O God, and we shall be healed;
save us, and we shall be saved; grant us
a perfect healing for all our infirmities.
We praise You, O God,
Healer of the sick.

רְפָאֵנוּ יי וְנֵרָפֵא, הוֹשִׁיעֵנוּ
וְנִוָּשֵׁעָה, וְהַעֲלֵה רְפוּאָה שְׁלֵמָה
לְכָל־מַכּוֹתֵינוּ.
בָּרוּךְ אַתָּה יי, רוֹפֵא הַחוֹלִים.

For Abundance

Bless this year for us, Eternal God;
may its produce bring us well-being.
Bestow Your blessing on the earth, that
all Your children may share its
abundance in peace.
We praise You, O God, for You bless
earth's seasons from year to year.

בָּרֵךְ עָלֵינוּ, יי אֱלֹהֵינוּ,
אֶת־הַשָּׁנָה הַזֹּאת וְאֶת־כָּל־מִינֵי
תְבוּאָתָהּ לְטוֹבָה. וְתֵן בְּרָכָה
עַל־פְּנֵי הָאֲדָמָה, וְשַׂבְּעֵנוּ מִטּוּבֶךָ.
בָּרוּךְ אַתָּה יי, מְבָרֵךְ הַשָּׁנִים.

For Freedom

Sound the great shofar to proclaim
freedom,
raise high the banner of liberation for
the oppressed,
and let the song of liberty be heard in
the four corners of the earth.
We praise You, O God, who loves
righteousness and justice.

תְּקַע בְּשׁוֹפָר גָּדוֹל לְחֵרוּתֵנוּ,
וְשָׂא נֵס לִפְדּוֹת עֲשׁוּקֵינוּ, וְקוֹל
דְּרוֹר יִשָּׁמַע בְּאַרְבַּע כַּנְפוֹת
הָאָרֶץ.
בָּרוּךְ אַתָּה יי, פּוֹדֶה עֲשׁוּקִים.

In each of the squares below, write down *one* thought from the prayer book that you think is important to the world.	Write down *why* you think each thought from the prayer book is important to the world.	Give some *examples of what people would need to do* to make that thought from the prayer book happen in today's world.

Group 3: The World Stands on Acts of Loving-Kindness

עַל גְּמִילוּת חֲסָדִים

The third important thing that Shimon HaTzadik said the world stood upon are acts of loving-kindness. These are things that people do to help one another. Spend a few minutes looking through some current newspapers or magazines to find articles describing people who show עַל גְּמִילוּת חֲסָדִים. Hint: You might also get some ideas from reading the Torah and prayer texts that groups 1 and 2 are working with. Then fill in the chart below.

From your readings, make a list of the things that people do to help one another.	Brainstorm other kind things that people can do for one another.	Brainstorm a list of reasons why you think גְּמִילוּת חֲסָדִים is important to the world.

An Ending Thought from You

Shimon HaTzadik said that the world stood on three things: on Torah, on worship, and on acts of loving-kindness. Rabban Shimon ben Gamliel offered three different ideas: truth, justice, and peace. We could write each of their ideas in a "Three Thoughts Triangle" that looks like this:

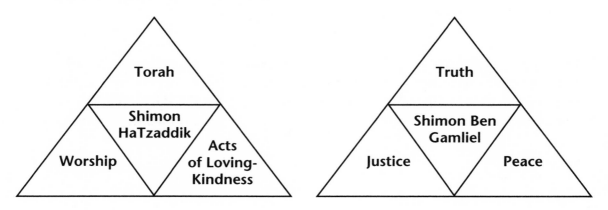

 What would be in your "Three Thoughts Triangle"? Write your name in the middle and then put your three ideas in the corners.

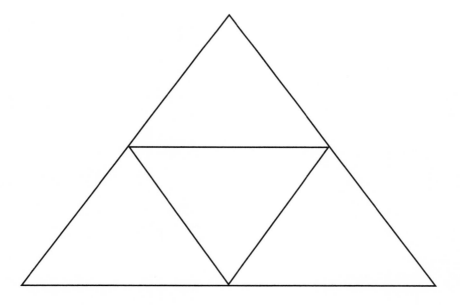

DON'T JUST SIT THERE!

4:5

Rabbi Yishmael … said	רַבִּי יִשְׁמָעֵאל … אוֹמֵר
"The one who studies in order to teach	הַלוֹמֵד עַל מְנָת לְלַמֵּד
will be enabled to study and to teach.	מַסְפִּיקִין בְּיָדוֹ לִלְמוֹד וּלְלַמֵּד.
The one who studies	וְהַלוֹמֵד עַל מְנָת
in order to practice,	לַעֲשׂוֹת
will be enabled	מַסְפִּיקִין בְּיָדוֹ
to study,	לִלְמוֹד
to teach,	וּלְלַמֵּד
to observe,	לִשְׁמוֹר
and to practice."	וְלַעֲשׂוֹת.

1:17

[Rabban Gamliel's] son Shimon said…	שִׁמְעוֹן בְּנוֹ אוֹמֵר...
"Study [of the Torah] is not the main thing;	וְלֹא הַמִּדְרָשׁ עִקָּר
[the] doing [of Torah] is."	אֶלָּא הַמַּעֲשֶׂה.

1:15

Shammai said…

"Say little,

but do much."

שַׁמַּאי אוֹמֵר...

אֱמוֹר מְעַט

וַעֲשֵׂה הַרְבֵּה....

A Beginning Thought: Don't just sit there, do something!

At some point in almost every Jewish child's life, he or she has asked, "Why do I have to go to religious school?" But, as you probably know, Jews put a lot of emphasis on education. We want our children to understand the specialness of being Jewish, the values of our religion, and the contributions of Jews to the world. The rabbis quoted above—and many others like them—tell us that learning has a purpose: We learn in order to do!

Take a few moments and brainstorm a list of the things you have learned to do as a Jew:

_____   _____

_____   _____

_____   _____

_____   _____

_____   _____

_____   _____

Thinking about Rabbi Yishmael's Ideas: Studying, Teaching, Observing, and Doing

Rabbi Yishmael offers the idea that one thing leads to another.

- A person can study.
- *Or*, a person can study to be able to teach.
- *Or*, a person can study to be able to "do!"

 With a partner, match these examples with Rabbi Yishmael's words. Write the letter of your choice in the space after each paragraph. Each choice may be used more than once.

1. Yael works as a teaching assistant in the first grade of her religious school. Each week at home, she makes sure to read the part of the Torah the students will be learning in class. _____

2. After her bat mitzvah, Dina decided to volunteer to chant Torah four more times during the year. She asked her cantor to teach her the trope tunes that were not part of her bat mitzvah portion. _____

3. Zac learned Torah trope so he could chant the Torah at his bar mitzvah.

   _____

4. At age fourteen, Caleb signed up for a special Torah trope class taught by his cantor. He reviewed the trope and learned some techniques for teaching it to sixth graders in his school. _____

5. Adam decides he wants to be a cantor. He asks his cantor to teach him how to lead the prayers of the Torah service.

   _____

A. The one who studies in order to teach will be able to study and to teach.

B. The one who studies in order to practice, will be enabled to study, to teach, to observe, and to practice.

Thinking about Shimon's Idea: Do Torah!

Shimon, the son of Rabban Gamliel, tells us that while it is important to study Torah, it is even more important to practice what we learn.

Many times we know exactly how we should behave according to Jewish tradition. For example, it is pretty easy to understand the basic idea behind "do not steal!" It means that we are not to take the property of others. But there are other things we can steal.

Sometimes we study the Torah and can't immediately see what the ideas have to do with us today. But Shimon, the son of Gamliel, tells us that taking action is more important than studying the idea. In his own words, he is telling us that study leads to action.

Work in a group of three or four students. Read the text below and then answer the questions that follow.

> YOU SHALL NOT SEE YOUR NEIGHBOR'S OX OR SHEEP WANDER AWAY AND IGNORE THEM. YOU MUST BRING THEM BACK TO YOUR NEIGHBOR. AND IF YOUR NEIGHBOR IS NOT NEAR YOU AND YOU DON'T KNOW WHO YOUR NEIGHBOR IS, THEN YOU MUST TAKE THE LOST ANIMAL TO YOUR HOME AND CARE FOR IT UNTIL YOUR NEIGHBOR CLAIMS IT, AND THEN YOU SHALL GIVE IT BACK. YOU MUST DO THE SAME FOR YOUR NEIGHBOR'S DONKEY, OR PIECE OF CLOTHING, OR ANYTHING THAT YOUR NEIGHBOR LOSES AND WHICH YOU FIND. YOU MAY NOT HIDE FROM RESPONSIBILITY.
>
> DEUTERONOMY 22:1–3

1. Check to make sure that each of you understands the words and phrases of this text. Define words or explain ideas that are unclear to someone.

2. If you find something that your neighbor lost, what does the Torah say you are supposed to do with it?

   _____

   _____

3. What other examples can you give that might fit this law?

   _____

   _____

4. "Your neighbor" does not just mean someone who lives next door to you. Who else might be defined as a neighbor?

   _____

   _____

5. What are other ways people hide from responsibility in today's world?

_____

_____

6. What would Rabbi Shimon tell you to do after you study this text from the Torah? Remember that he said, "Study [of the Torah] is not the main thing; [the] doing [of Torah] is."

_____

_____

Thinking About Shammai's Idea: Say Little, Do Much!

There is a story by I. L. Peretz, a Yiddish writer from about 100 years ago, called "If Not Higher." It takes place in a small shtetl (town or village) in eastern Europe during the High Holy Days. Each year the rabbi is missing from the synagogue during some of the most important and holiest prayers. The townspeople are convinced that the rabbi is absent because he is in heaven discussing with God the fine merits of his people.

One year, a man visits the town. He does not believe that the rabbi goes high up to heaven to talk to God, and so he decides to find out once and for all where the rabbi is when he should be in synagogue. One night the man hides under the rabbi's bed and watches in amazement to see the rabbi awake before dawn and dress in dirty, torn peasant clothing. The rabbi throws an axe over his shoulder and walks to the home of a very poor sick person; the man quietly follows. The rabbi first chops wood and then makes a fire to warm the sick person, all the time quietly chanting the prayers.

Ultimately, the man who once wanted to catch the rabbi doing something wrong becomes one of the rabbi's biggest supporters. Years after, when the townspeople would say that their rabbi was up in heaven talking to God on their behalf, the man would respond, "If not higher."

Talk with a friend about the story and together explain how it is a good example of Shammai's statement, "Say little, but do much."

_____

_____

_____

_____

_____

An Ending Thought from You

There are students who study hard, learn what teachers ask them to, and do well on written tests—but behave badly in life. The three rabbis studied in this lesson tell us that it's important to learn about Judaism so that we act properly in our lives. We must "take action." Think about the many ideas you have learned while studying this book (you might want to look back through past chapters). What will you *do?*

Brainstorm a list of ways you can live your life as a committed Jew who takes action in the world.

_____

_____

_____

_____

_____

_____

NOW IS THE TIME!

2:15

Rabbi Tarfon said,

    "The day is short.

    There is much work [to be done]."

רַבִּי טַרְפוֹן אוֹמֵר

הַיּוֹם קָצָר

וְהַמְּלָאכָה מְרֻבָּה.

2:16

He used to say,

    "It is not up to you to finish the work,

    but you are not free
    to avoid it."

הוּא הָיָה אוֹמֵר

לֹא עָלֶיךָ הַמְּלָאכָה לִגְמוֹר

וְלֹא אַתָּה בֶן חוֹרִין
לְהִבָּטֵל מִמֶּנָּה.

A Beginning Thought: Now Is The Time!

There are many demands on our time. It may feel impossible to find the time to take action.

"I have too much work to do!"

"I can't do it!"

"I am overwhelmed!"

1. When have you felt like there is too much work to do?_____

_____

2. How have you handled the situation?
   - ☐ Given up
   - ☐ Found a small piece I could handle
   - ☐ Taken lots of time to do it all
   - ☐ Found someone who could help me

   ☐ _____

The Day Is Short, There Is Much Work

The phrase above is rather brief; it feels as if something is missing. And, indeed, there is. The full מִשְׁנָה says,

> THE DAY IS SHORT, THERE IS MUCH WORK [TO BE DONE]; [YET], THE
> LABORERS ARE LAZY, [EVEN THOUGH] THE WAGES ARE GREAT AND THE
> EMPLOYER IS INSISTENT.

In reading the full מִשְׁנָה, however, one might still ask what Rabbi Tarfon *is* trying to say. With two other people, take a few minutes to write out questions that you would want to ask Rabbi Tarfon so that you could better understand his message.

1. _____

_____

2. _____

_____

3. _____

_____

4. _____

_____

and   Join with another group of three and consider how Rabbi Tarfon might answer your questions. What do you think Rabbi Tarfon is trying to tell us? (Or, why does it matter that "the day is short and there is much work"?)

_____

_____

_____

_____

_____

Why It Matters

If a teacher said to you, "The day is short and there is much work to be done," you would probably realize that you'd better focus on your assignment—otherwise the leftover work might become homework!

Think about Rabbi Tarfon's statement in a variety of situations. In each case, why does it matter that the day is short and there is much work to be done?

metaphor

A word or phrase that gives an image of an idea, instead of describing the thought directly. In this example, workers are a metaphor for humans and the employer is a metaphor for God.

Many people think that Rabbi Tarfon gives his advice with God on his mind. The workers (human beings) are lazy but the employer (God) is going to insist we get our work done!

• In this **metaphor**, what *work* does God want us to get done? _____

_____

• In this metaphor, what are the *great wages* for getting this work done?

_____

_____

_____

What if the Work Feels Overwhelming?

Rabbi Tarfon realized that simply saying "the day is short and there is much work" may make a person feel overwhelmed. Here is an example:

> MIRIAM'S CLASS HAS DECIDED IT WANTS TO HELP PEOPLE WHO DO NOT HAVE ENOUGH TO EAT. IN CLASS, THEY BRAINSTORM A LIST OF THINGS THEY CAN DO.

> DO A CANNED FOOD DRIVE.
> SERVE A MEAL AT A SOUP KITCHEN.
> COLLECT MONEY TO DONATE TO MAZON: A JEWISH RESPONSE TO HUNGER.
> ASK FAMILIES WHO CELEBRATE EVENTS IN THE SYNAGOGUE TO DONATE LEFTOVER FOOD TO A LOCAL SOUP KITCHEN.
> FIGURE OUT HOW TO HELP IN PUBLIC SCHOOLS THAT HAVE A LARGE NUMBER OF POOR PEOPLE TO GET MORE FREE BREAKFASTS.

> AT ONE POINT, A STUDENT IN THE CLASS SAYS, "THERE'S SO MUCH TO DO! WE'LL NEVER BE ABLE TO HELP ALL THE PEOPLE WHO DON'T HAVE ENOUGH TO EAT!"

Take a look at one more saying of Rabbi Tarfon:

> IT IS NOT UP TO YOU TO FINISH THE WORK, BUT NEITHER ARE YOU FREE TO AVOID IT.

If Miriam and her classmates remember this advice, what might they do once they finished brainstorming their list?

_____

_____

_____

_____

_____

An Ending Thought from You

Our lives can be overwhelmingly full. We run from activity to activity, we have lots of schoolwork to do, and we also want to hang out with our friends.

- What is one thing you have wanted to do, but for which you have so far not been able to make the time?

_____

_____

- If not now, when? How will you make the time?

_____

_____

Unit Wrap-Up

פִּרְקֵי אָבוֹת on Taking Action

Don't just stand there, do something!

This book took you on a journey into the past. You studied the religious ideas of rabbis who lived 2,000 years ago but whose wisdom is helpful to us today. A person could get overwhelmed trying to follow all their advice. But while we can't do it all, we must do what is in our power.

At the end of the last chapter, you brainstormed a list of some of the things you might do as an active, committed Jew. Now it's time to *make* a commitment!

Take some time to review the advice of the rabbis in פִּרְקֵי אָבוֹת. Choose one statement that you would be willing to make part of your life, then make a commitment to take action, based upon this advice given 2,000 years ago.

I believe that one of the most important pieces of advice from פִּרְקֵי אָבוֹת *is*

_____

_____

_____

_____.

*by Rabbi*_____

I think that this is important advice because _____

_____

_____

_____

_____.

And so, I promise to _____

_____

_____

_____.

Signed,

_____

Date _____

ENGLISH GLOSSARY

associate

The Hebrew word is חָבֵר *(chaver)*, or friend. The translator used the word "associate" to mean someone who is equal to you (for example, a business associate).

bereaved

A person who is sad that someone he or she loved has died.

characteristic

A specific quality in a person.

desire

To want or wish for something.

despise

To think of something as worthless; to scorn.

disgraced

A person who feels shame or who has lost honor. A disgraced person often feels embarrassed.

empathy

A person's ability to understand the feelings of someone else.

entrepreneur

A person who takes a risk starting up a new business.

envy

To resent someone else's achievements or possessions.

lightly esteemed

Not valued; held in low regard.

metaphor

A word or phrase that gives an image of an idea, instead of describing the thought directly.

priesthood

In the Torah, God commands Aaron and his family to serve as the כֹּהֲנִים *(kohanim)*, or priests, taking care of the rituals in the Tabernacle in the desert, and later at the Temple in Jerusalem. This service is called the priesthood.

reputable

Something (or someone) with a good reputation; known to be honest or trustworthy.

reverence

Respect. The Hebrew word, מוֹרָא *(morah)*, is translated as "respect" the other times it is used here.

rhetorical

Used to describe a question or statement that does not need a response. The person asking it is doing it to make a point and usually believes that there is only one correct answer to the question, and that the people listening know it too.

role model

Someone who influences our lives. This person models actions and ideas that we find important enough to do ourselves.

Sodom kind

This refers to the kind of behavior shown by the people of Sodom and Gomorrah, the two towns God destroyed (see Genesis 18–19).

temperament

General way in which a person handles emotions and approaches life.

HEBREW GLOSSARY

אֲרוֹן הַקֹּדֶשׁ

The Holy Ark *(Aron HaKodesh)*, found in each synagogue.

בְּצֶלֶם אֱלֹהִים

In the image of God *(b'tzelem Elohim)*.

גֹּלֶם

Shapeless mass or embryo *(golem)*; the name of a very famous Jewish "monster" reportedly brought to life by a rabbi. Used as "fool."

הַכֹּהֵן הַגָּדוֹל

The High Priest *(HaKohen HaGadol)*, the title of the person in charge of the ritual in the Tabernacle in the desert and later at the Temple in Jerusalem.

כֶּתֶר שֵׁם טוֹב

"Crown of a good name."
crown = כֶּתֶר *(keter)*
name = שֵׁם *(shem)*
good = טוֹב *(tov)*

מִדְרָשׁ (Midrash)

A story that helps explain something unclear in the Bible. A *midrash* usually fills in a hole that the Bible leaves open. (The plural form is *midrashim.*)

מִשְׁנָה (Mishnah)

A small piece of text, like a verse from the Bible, but found in the Jewish books known as the Mishnah and the Talmud, which were written more than 1,500 years ago. In this worktext, the word מִשְׁנָה will appear in Hebrew when referring to the small piece of text. When referring to the book, the English "Mishnah," will be used.

פִּרְקֵי אָבוֹת

Pirkei Avot.

שָׁלוֹם עָלֶיךָ רַבִּי

"Peace to you, my teacher." *(Shalom alecha rahbi.)*

שָׁלוֹם עָלֶיךָ רַבִּי רַבִּי, מוֹרִי מוֹרִי

"Peace to you, my rabbi my rabbi, my teacher my teacher." *(Shalom alecha rahbi rahbi, mori mori.)*

שֵׁם טוֹב

Good name *(shem tov)*.

צְדָקָה

(Tzedakah); an obligation to give money to others to help them fulfill their basic needs.

Chapter 1

1.1 At Sinai Moses received the Torah and handed it over to Joshua who handed it over to the elders who handed it over to the prophets who in turn handed it over to the men of the Great Assembly. The latter said three things: Be deliberate in judgment, raise up many disciples, and make a fence around the Torah.

1:2 Simon the Righteous was one of the last of the Great Assembly. His motto was: "The world stands on three things–The Torah, the [Temple] service, and loving acts of kindness."

1:3 Antigonos of Socho received [the Tradition] from Simon the Righteous. His motto was: "Don't be like those who would serve a master on the condition that they would receive a reward. Rather, be like those who would serve without that condition. Even so, let the fear of Heaven be upon you."

1:4 Yose ben Yoezer of Zeredah and Yose ben Yochanan of Jerusalem received [the Tradition] from them. Yose ben Yoezer said, "Let your house be a meeting place for the wise; sit humbly at their feet; and, with thirst, drink in their words."

1:5 Yose ben Yochanan of Jerusalem said, "Let your house be open wide; let the poor be members of your household; and don't talk to your wife too much." They said that about his own wife, how much the more another man's wife. From this [statement] other sages said: "When a man talks too much to his wife, he causes evil to himself, disregards the words of the Torah, and in the end will inherit Gehinnom."

1:6 Joshua ben Perachyah and Nittai of Arbel received [the Tradition] from them. Joshua ben Perachyah said, "Get yourself a teacher, find someone to study with, and judge everyone favorably."

1:7 Nittai of Arbel said, "Keep your distance from an evil neighbor; don't be the buddy of a wicked person; and don't give up on [the reality of] retribution."

1:8 Judah ben Tabbai and Shimon ben Shetach received [the Tradition] from them. Judah ben Tabbai said, "[When you are a judge] don't play the advocate's role. When the litigants stand before you, let them appear to you equally culpable. When they leave you, having accepted judgment, let them look equally blameless to you."

1:9 Shimon ben Shetach said, "Ask many questions of the witnesses, but be very careful what you say [to them], lest from your words, they [the witnesses] learn to perjure [themselves]."

1:10 Shemayah and Avtalyon received [the Tradition] from them. Shemayah said, "Love labor, hate [the abuse of] power, and don't try to become the familiar friend of government."

פרק א

א מֹשֶׁה קִבֵּל תּוֹרָה מִסִּינַי, וּמְסָרָהּ לִיהוֹשֻׁעַ, וִיהוֹשֻׁעַ לִזְקֵנִים, וּזְקֵנִים לִנְבִיאִים, וּנְבִיאִים מְסָרוּהָ לְאַנְשֵׁי כְנֶסֶת הַגְּדוֹלָה. הֵם אָמְרוּ שְׁלשָׁה דְבָרִים, הֱווּ מְתוּנִים בַּדִּין, וְהַעֲמִידוּ תַלְמִידִים הַרְבֵּה, וַעֲשׂוּ סְיָג לַתּוֹרָה:

ב שִׁמְעוֹן הַצַּדִּיק הָיָה מִשְּׁיָרֵי כְנֶסֶת הַגְּדוֹלָה. הוּא הָיָה אוֹמֵר, עַל שְׁלשָׁה דְבָרִים הָעוֹלָם עוֹמֵד, עַל הַתּוֹרָה וְעַל הָעֲבוֹדָה וְעַל גְּמִילוּת חֲסָדִים:

ג אַנְטִיגְנוֹס אִישׁ סוֹכוֹ קִבֵּל מִשִּׁמְעוֹן הַצַּדִּיק. הוּא הָיָה אוֹמֵר, אַל תִּהְיוּ כַעֲבָדִים הַמְשַׁמְּשִׁין אֶת הָרַב עַל מְנָת לְקַבֵּל פְּרָס, אֶלָּא הֱווּ כַעֲבָדִים הַמְשַׁמְּשִׁין אֶת הָרַב שֶׁלֹּא עַל מְנָת לְקַבֵּל פְּרָס, וִיהִי מוֹרָא שָׁמַיִם עֲלֵיכֶם:

ד יוֹסֵי בֶּן יוֹעֶזֶר אִישׁ צְרֵדָה וְיוֹסֵי בֶּן יוֹחָנָן אִישׁ יְרוּשָׁלַיִם קִבְּלוּ מֵהֶם. יוֹסֵי בֶּן יוֹעֶזֶר אִישׁ צְרֵדָה אוֹמֵר, יְהִי בֵיתְךָ בֵית וַעַד לַחֲכָמִים, וֶהֱוֵי מִתְאַבֵּק בַּעֲפַר רַגְלֵיהֶם, וֶהֱוֵי שׁוֹתֶה בַצָּמָא אֶת דִּבְרֵיהֶם:

ה יוֹסֵי בֶּן יוֹחָנָן אִישׁ יְרוּשָׁלַיִם אוֹמֵר, יְהִי בֵיתְךָ פָתוּחַ לִרְוָחָה, וְיִהְיוּ עֲנִיִּים בְּנֵי בֵיתֶךָ, וְאַל תַּרְבֶּה שִׂיחָה עִם הָאִשָּׁה. בְּאִשְׁתּוֹ אָמְרוּ, קַל וָחֹמֶר בְּאֵשֶׁת חֲבֵרוֹ. מִכָּאן אָמְרוּ חֲכָמִים, כָּל זְמַן שֶׁאָדָם מַרְבֶּה שִׂיחָה עִם הָאִשָּׁה, גּוֹרֵם רָעָה לְעַצְמוֹ, וּבוֹטֵל מִדִּבְרֵי תוֹרָה, וְסוֹפוֹ יוֹרֵשׁ גֵּיהִנָּם:

ו יְהוֹשֻׁעַ בֶּן פְּרַחְיָה וְנִתַּאי הָאַרְבֵּלִי קִבְּלוּ מֵהֶם. יְהוֹשֻׁעַ בֶּן פְּרַחְיָה אוֹמֵר, עֲשֵׂה לְךָ רַב, וּקְנֵה לְךָ חָבֵר, וֶהֱוֵי דָן אֶת כָּל הָאָדָם לְכַף זְכוּת:

ז נִתַּאי הָאַרְבֵּלִי אוֹמֵר, הַרְחֵק מִשָּׁכֵן רָע, וְאַל תִּתְחַבֵּר לָרָשָׁע, וְאַל תִּתְיָאֵשׁ מִן הַפֻּרְעָנוּת:

ח יְהוּדָה בֶּן טַבַּאי וְשִׁמְעוֹן בֶּן שָׁטַח קִבְּלוּ מֵהֶם. יְהוּדָה בֶּן טַבַּאי אוֹמֵר, אַל תַּעַשׂ עַצְמְךָ כְּעוֹרְכֵי הַדַּיָּנִין. וּכְשֶׁיִּהְיוּ בַעֲלֵי דִינִין עוֹמְדִים לְפָנֶיךָ, יִהְיוּ בְעֵינֶיךָ כִרְשָׁעִים, וּכְשֶׁנִּפְטָרִים מִלְּפָנֶיךָ, יִהְיוּ בְעֵינֶיךָ כְזַכָּאִין, כְּשֶׁקִּבְּלוּ עֲלֵיהֶם אֶת הַדִּין:

ט שִׁמְעוֹן בֶּן שָׁטַח אוֹמֵר, הֱוֵי מַרְבֶּה לַחֲקֹר אֶת הָעֵדִים, וֶהֱוֵי זָהִיר בִּדְבָרֶיךָ, שֶׁמָּא מִתּוֹכָם יִלְמְדוּ לְשַׁקֵּר:

י שְׁמַעְיָה וְאַבְטַלְיוֹן קִבְּלוּ מֵהֶם. שְׁמַעְיָה אוֹמֵר, אֱהֹב אֶת הַמְּלָאכָה, וּשְׂנָא אֶת הָרַבָּנוּת, וְאַל תִּתְוַדַּע לָרָשׁוּת:

1:11 Avtalyon said, "Sages, watch your words, lest you be punished by exile to a place of bad water, and lest your students, who follow after you, drink and die and, as a result, cause the name of Heaven to be profaned."

1:12 Hillel and Shammai received [the Tradition] from them. Hillel said, "Be one of Aaron's students, loving peace and pursuing it, loving people and bringing them to the Torah."

1:13 He used to say, "A name made great is a name destroyed; one who does not increase decreases; one who will not study deserves to die: one who makes [illicit] use of the Torah will perish."

1:14 He used to say, "If I am not for myself, who will be for me? And, if I am for myself alone, then what am I? And, if not now, when?"

1:15 Shammai said, "Make your Torah [study] a habit; say little, but do much; and greet every person cheerfully."

1:16 Rabban Gamliel said, "Get yourself a teacher; avoid doubt; and don't guess when you tithe."

1:17 His son Shimon said, "I have grown up among the sages all my days, yet I have never found anything better than silence. Study [of the Torah] is not the main thing; [the] doing [of Torah] is. All who talk too much bring sin."

1:18 Rabban Shimon, the son of Gamliel, said, "The world stands on three things: on truth, on judgment, and on peace; as it is stated [in Scripture]: 'Execute the judgment of truth and peace in your gates.'" [Zech. 8:16]

Chapter 2

2:1 Rabbi [Yehudah Ha-Nasi] was fond of saying: "Which is the proper path [of life] that one should select? The one that seems honorable for oneself and brings honor [bestowed by] others. Be as careful in the performance of [an ostensibly] minor commandment as [what seems to be] a major commandment, since you do not know the [potential] reward for [the performance of any of] the commandments. Compute the loss in doing a commandment against its reward and the benefit of a transgression against what will be lost. Think deeply about three things and you will never be gripped by the desire to commit a transgression. Know what is above you: an eye that sees, an ear that hears, and all your deeds are inscribed in a book.

2:2 Rabban Gamliel, the son of Rabbi Yehudah Ha-Nasi, said, "It is good to join the study of Torah to some kind of work for the effort required by both robs sin of power. Torah study without work will end up being useless and will cause sin. Let all who work with the congregation do so for the sake of Heaven; the merit of their ancestors will

יא אַבְטַלְיוֹן אוֹמֵר, חֲכָמִים, הִזָּהֲרוּ בְדִבְרֵיכֶם, שֶׁמָּא תָחוֹבוּ חוֹבַת גָּלוּת וְתִגְלוּ לִמְקוֹם מַיִם הָרָעִים, וְיִשְׁתּוּ הַתַּלְמִידִים הַבָּאִים אַחֲרֵיכֶם וְיָמוּתוּ, וְנִמְצָא שֵׁם שָׁמַיִם מִתְחַלֵּל:

יב הִלֵּל וְשַׁמַּאי קִבְּלוּ מֵהֶם. הִלֵּל אוֹמֵר, הֱוֵי מִתַּלְמִידָיו שֶׁל אַהֲרֹן אוֹהֵב שָׁלוֹם וְרוֹדֵף שָׁלוֹם, אוֹהֵב אֶת הַבְּרִיּוֹת וּמְקָרְבָן לַתּוֹרָה:

יג הוּא הָיָה אוֹמֵר, נְגַד שְׁמָא, אֲבַד שְׁמֵהּ. וּדְלָא מוֹסִיף, יָסֵיף. וּדְלָא יָלֵיף, קְטָלָא חַיָּב. וּדְאִשְׁתַּמֵּשׁ בְּתַגָּא, חֲלָף:

יד הוּא הָיָה אוֹמֵר, אִם אֵין אֲנִי לִי, מִי לִי. וּכְשֶׁאֲנִי לְעַצְמִי, מָה אֲנִי. וְאִם לֹא עַכְשָׁיו, אֵימָתָי:

טו שַׁמַּאי אוֹמֵר, עֲשֵׂה תוֹרָתְךָ קֶבַע. אֱמוֹר מְעַט וַעֲשֵׂה הַרְבֵּה, וֶהֱוֵי מְקַבֵּל אֶת כָּל הָאָדָם בְּסֵבֶר פָּנִים יָפוֹת:

טז רַבָּן גַּמְלִיאֵל הָיָה אוֹמֵר, עֲשֵׂה לְךָ רַב, וְהִסְתַּלֵּק מִן הַסָּפֵק, וְאַל תַּרְבֶּה לְעַשֵּׂר אֲמָדוֹת:

יז שִׁמְעוֹן בְּנוֹ אוֹמֵר, כָּל יָמַי גָּדַלְתִּי בֵּין הַחֲכָמִים, וְלֹא מָצָאתִי לַגּוּף טוֹב אֶלָּא שְׁתִיקָה. וְלֹא הַמִּדְרָשׁ הוּא הָעִקָּר, אֶלָּא הַמַּעֲשֶׂה. וְכָל הַמַּרְבֶּה דְבָרִים, מֵבִיא חֵטְא:

יח רַבָּן שִׁמְעוֹן בֶּן גַּמְלִיאֵל אוֹמֵר, עַל שְׁלשָׁה דְבָרִים הָעוֹלָם עוֹמֵד, עַל הַדִּין וְעַל הָאֱמֶת וְעַל הַשָּׁלוֹם, שֶׁנֶּאֱמַר (זכריה ח) אֱמֶת וּמִשְׁפַּט שָׁלוֹם שִׁפְטוּ בְּשַׁעֲרֵיכֶם:

פרק ב

א רַבִּי אוֹמֵר, אֵיזוֹהִי דֶרֶךְ יְשָׁרָה שֶׁיָּבוֹר לוֹ הָאָדָם, כֹּל שֶׁהִיא תִפְאֶרֶת לְעוֹשֶׂיהָ וְתִפְאֶרֶת לוֹ מִן הָאָדָם. וֶהֱוֵי זָהִיר בְּמִצְוָה קַלָּה כְּבַחֲמוּרָה, שֶׁאֵין אַתָּה יוֹדֵעַ מַתַּן שְׂכָרָן שֶׁל מִצְוֹת. וֶהֱוֵי מְחַשֵּׁב הֶפְסֵד מִצְוָה כְּנֶגֶד שְׂכָרָהּ, וּשְׂכַר עֲבֵרָה כְּנֶגֶד הֶפְסֵדָהּ. וְהִסְתַּכֵּל בִּשְׁלשָׁה דְבָרִים וְאִי אַתָּה בָא לִידֵי עֲבֵרָה, דַּע מַה לְּמַעְלָה מִמְּךָ, עַיִן רוֹאָה וְאֹזֶן שׁוֹמַעַת, וְכָל מַעֲשֶׂיךָ בַּסֵּפֶר נִכְתָּבִין:

ב רַבָּן גַּמְלִיאֵל בְּנוֹ שֶׁל רַבִּי יְהוּדָה הַנָּשִׂיא אוֹמֵר, יָפֶה תַלְמוּד תּוֹרָה עִם דֶּרֶךְ אֶרֶץ, שֶׁיְּגִיעַת שְׁנֵיהֶם מְשַׁכַּחַת עָוֹן. וְכָל תּוֹרָה שֶׁאֵין עִמָּהּ מְלָאכָה, סוֹפָהּ בְּטֵלָה וְגוֹרֶרֶת עָוֹן. וְכָל הָעֲמֵלִים עִם הַצִּבּוּר,

sustain them and, as a result, their righteousness will remain forever." As for you [God says], "I will credit you with a great reward, as if you had accomplished it all."

2:3 Watch out for the government: They befriend a person to meet their own needs, appearing friendly when it is to their benefit; but they do not stand by a person when that person is in distress.

2:4 This was his motto: "Do God's will as if it were your own, so that God may do your will as God's own will. Adapt your will to God's will, so that God may change the will of others instead of yours." Hillel said, "Don't separate yourself from the community. Don't be over-confident until the day of your death. Don't judge your fellow human being until you have reached that person's place. Don't say anything that is unintelligible with the hope that it will be understood. And don't say, 'When I have leisure, I will study'–perhaps, you never will have that leisure."

2:5 Another of his [Hillel's] mottos: "The brute will not fear sin. The ignoramus will not be saintly. The inhibited will not learn. The irate cannot teach. Nor can one given over to business grow wise. In a place where there are no human beings, try to be one."

2:6 He once saw a skull floating on the surface of the water. He said to it, "Because you drowned people, others drowned you. They in turn will be drowned by others."

2:7 He used to say, "The more flesh, the more worms; the more possessions, the more worry; the more wives, the more witchcraft; the more maidservants, the more lewdness; the more menservants, the more theft; the more Torah, the more life; the more schooling, the more wisdom; the more counsel, the more understanding; the more righteous charity, the more peace. One who has acquired a good name has acquired it for oneself. One who has acquired the words of Torah has acquired for oneself a place in the world to come."

2:8 Rabban Yochanan ben Zakkai received [the Tradition] from Hillel and from Shammai. He would say, "If you have learned much Torah, don't take the credit, for it was for that purpose that you were created." Rabban Yochanan ben Zakkai had five students. They were Rabbi Eliezer ben Horkenos, Rabbi Yehoshua ben Chananya, Rabbi Yose Ha-Kohen, Rabbi Shimon ben Netanel, and Rabbi Elazar ben Arach. He would [often] recount their merits [as follows]: "Rabbi Eliezer ben Horkenos is like a cemented cistern that does not lose a drop; as for Rabbi Yehoshua, 'Happy is she who bore him!'; Rabbi Yose is a pious man; Rabbi Shimon ben Netanel is one who fears sin; Rabbi Elazar ben Arach is [like] an evergushing spring." He [Rabbi Yochanan] would often say, "Were all the sages of Israel in one balance pan of a scale and Rabbi Eliezer ben Horkenos in the other, he [Rabbi Eliezer] would outweigh them all." Abba Shaul [remembered the teaching differently and] quoted him, "If

יִהְיוּ עֲמֵלִים עִמָּהֶם לְשֵׁם שָׁמַיִם, שֶׁזְּכוּת אֲבוֹתָם מְסַיַּעְתָּן וְצִדְקָתָם עוֹמֶדֶת לָעַד. וְאַתֶּם, מַעֲלֶה אֲנִי עֲלֵיכֶם שָׂכָר הַרְבֵּה כְּאִלּוּ עֲשִׂיתֶם:

ג הֱווּ זְהִירִין בָּרָשׁוּת, שֶׁאֵין מְקָרְבִין לוֹ לָאָדָם אֶלָּא לְצֹרֶךְ עַצְמָן. נִרְאִין כְּאוֹהֲבִין בִּשְׁעַת הֲנָאָתָן. וְאֵין עוֹמְדִין לוֹ לָאָדָם בִּשְׁעַת דָּחֳקוֹ:

ד הוּא הָיָה אוֹמֵר, עֲשֵׂה רְצוֹנוֹ כִּרְצוֹנֶךָ, כְּדֵי שֶׁיַּעֲשֶׂה רְצוֹנְךָ כִּרְצוֹנוֹ. בַּטֵּל רְצוֹנְךָ מִפְּנֵי רְצוֹנוֹ, כְּדֵי שֶׁיְּבַטֵּל רְצוֹן אֲחֵרִים מִפְּנֵי רְצוֹנֶךָ. הִלֵּל אוֹמֵר, אַל תִּפְרוֹשׁ מִן הַצִּבּוּר, וְאַל תַּאֲמֵן בְּעַצְמְךָ עַד יוֹם מוֹתְךָ, וְאַל תָּדִין אֶת חֲבֵרְךָ עַד שֶׁתַּגִּיעַ לִמְקוֹמוֹ, וְאַל תֹּאמַר דָּבָר שֶׁאִי אֶפְשָׁר לִשְׁמוֹעַ שֶׁסּוֹפוֹ לְהִשָּׁמַע. וְאַל תֹּאמַר לִכְשֶׁאֶפָּנֶה אֶשְׁנֶה, שֶׁמָּא לֹא תִפָּנֶה:

ה הוּא הָיָה אוֹמֵר, אֵין בּוּר יְרֵא חֵטְא, וְלֹא עַם הָאָרֶץ חָסִיד, וְלֹא הַבַּיְשָׁן לָמֵד, וְלֹא הַקַּפְּדָן מְלַמֵּד, וְלֹא כָל הַמַּרְבֶּה בִסְחוֹרָה מַחְכִּים. וּבִמְקוֹם שֶׁאֵין אֲנָשִׁים, הִשְׁתַּדֵּל לִהְיוֹת אִישׁ:

ו אַף הוּא רָאָה גֻלְגֹּלֶת אַחַת שֶׁצָּפָה עַל פְּנֵי הַמָּיִם. אָמַר (לָהּ), עַל דַּאֲטֵפְתְּ, אַטְפוּךְ. וְסוֹף מְטַיְפַיִךְ יְטוּפוּן:

ז הוּא הָיָה אוֹמֵר, מַרְבֶּה בָשָׂר, מַרְבֶּה רִמָּה. מַרְבֶּה נְכָסִים, מַרְבֶּה דְאָגָה. מַרְבֶּה נָשִׁים, מַרְבֶּה כְשָׁפִים. מַרְבֶּה שְׁפָחוֹת, מַרְבֶּה זִמָּה. מַרְבֶּה עֲבָדִים, מַרְבֶּה גָזֵל. מַרְבֶּה תוֹרָה, מַרְבֶּה חַיִּים. מַרְבֶּה יְשִׁיבָה, מַרְבֶּה חָכְמָה. מַרְבֶּה עֵצָה, מַרְבֶּה תְבוּנָה. מַרְבֶּה צְדָקָה, מַרְבֶּה שָׁלוֹם. קָנָה שֵׁם טוֹב, קָנָה לְעַצְמוֹ. קָנָה לוֹ דִבְרֵי תוֹרָה, קָנָה לוֹ חַיֵּי הָעוֹלָם הַבָּא:

ח רַבָּן יוֹחָנָן בֶּן זַכַּאי קִבֵּל מֵהִלֵּל וּמִשַּׁמַּאי. הוּא הָיָה אוֹמֵר, אִם לָמַדְתָּ תוֹרָה הַרְבֵּה, אַל תַּחֲזִיק טוֹבָה לְעַצְמְךָ, כִּי לְכָךְ נוֹצָרְתָּ. חֲמִשָּׁה תַלְמִידִים הָיוּ לוֹ לְרַבָּן יוֹחָנָן בֶּן זַכַּאי, וְאֵלּוּ הֵן, רַבִּי אֱלִיעֶזֶר בֶּן הֻרְקְנוֹס, וְרַבִּי יְהוֹשֻׁעַ בֶּן חֲנַנְיָה, וְרַבִּי יוֹסֵי הַכֹּהֵן, וְרַבִּי שִׁמְעוֹן בֶּן נְתַנְאֵל, וְרַבִּי אֶלְעָזָר בֶּן עֲרָךְ. הוּא הָיָה מוֹנֶה שְׁבָחָן. רַבִּי אֱלִיעֶזֶר בֶּן הֻרְקְנוֹס, בּוֹר סוּד שֶׁאֵינוֹ מְאַבֵּד טִפָּה. רַבִּי יְהוֹשֻׁעַ בֶּן חֲנַנְיָה, אַשְׁרֵי יוֹלַדְתּוֹ. רַבִּי יוֹסֵי הַכֹּהֵן, חָסִיד. רַבִּי שִׁמְעוֹן בֶּן נְתַנְאֵל, יְרֵא חֵטְא. וְרַבִּי אֶלְעָזָר בֶּן עֲרָךְ, מַעְיָן הַמִּתְגַּבֵּר. הוּא הָיָה אוֹמֵר, אִם יִהְיוּ כָל חַכְמֵי יִשְׂרָאֵל בְּכַף מֹאזְנַיִם, וֶאֱלִיעֶזֶר בֶּן הֻרְקְנוֹס בְּכַף שְׁנִיָּה, מַכְרִיעַ אֶת כֻּלָּם. אַבָּא שָׁאוּל אוֹמֵר מִשְּׁמוֹ, אִם יִהְיוּ כָל חַכְמֵי יִשְׂרָאֵל בְּכַף

all the sages of Israel including Rabbi Eliezer ben Horkenos were in one balance pan of a scale and Rabbi Elazar ben Arach in the other, he [Rabbi Elazar] would outweigh them all."

2:9 He [Rabbi Yochanan] said to them: "Go and see which way one should follow." Rabbi Eliezer said, "[One should have] a good eye." Rabbi Yehoshua said, "[One should be] a good friend." Rabbi Yose said, "[One should be] a good neighbor." Rabbi Shimon said, "[One should] anticipate the future." Rabbi Elazar said, "[One should have] a good heart." Rabbi Yochanan responded, "I prefer Rabbi Elazar's answer to all of the other answers because it contains all of the others." [Rabbi Yochanan] then said, "Go out and see from what should one flee?" Rabbi Eliezer said, "[Having] an evil eye." Rabbi Yehoshua said, "[Being] a bad neighbor." Rabbi Shimon said, "[Being] one who borrows and does not repay. Whether one borrows from a neighbor or from God, it is the same, as it is written, 'The wicked borrow and do not repay, while the righteous graciously give.'" [Ps. 37:21] Rabbi Elazar said, "[Having] an evil heart." Rabbi Yochanan responded, "I prefer Rabbi Elazar's answer. All of your answers are included in his statement."

2:10 They each said three things. Rabbi Eliezer said, "Let your friend's honor be as precious to you as your own. Be difficult to provoke. And repent one day before your death." [He also said], "Warm yourself by the fire of the sages, but take care that you don't get burned by their coals. Their bite is the bite of a fox; their sting is a scorpion stinging; and their hiss is a viper hiss. Indeed, all their words are like coals of fire."

2:11 Rabbi Yehoshua said, "The evil eye, the evil urge, and hatred of [one's fellow] creatures take one out of the world."

2:12 Rabbi Yose would say, "Let your friend's property be as dear to you as your own. Since you cannot inherit the Torah, you must prepare yourself to study it. Let all that you do be for the sake of Heaven."

2:13 Rabbi Shimon said, "Be very careful in reciting the *Shema* and the *Tefilah*. When you pray, don't make your prayer a fixed form, but rather [infuse it with] a plea for mercy and grace before God, as Scripture teaches, 'For God is a compassionate and gracious God, long suffering and abounding in steadfast love and relenting of evil.' [Joel 2:13] [Moreover] don't be wicked in your own mind."

2:14 Rabbi Elazar would say, "Study the Torah diligently. Know how to answer the nonbeliever. And know in whose presence you work and how dependable your Employer is to pay your wage."

2:15 Rabbi Tarfon used to say, "The day is short; there is much work [to be done]; [yet,] the laborers are lazy, [even though] the wages are great and the Householder is insistent."

2:16 He would say, "It is not up to you to finish the work,

מַאֲזְנַיִם וְרַבִּי אֱלִיעֶזֶר בֶּן הֻרְקְנוֹס אַף עִמָּהֶם, וְרַבִּי אֶלְעָזָר בֶּן עֲרָךְ בְּכַף שְׁנִיָּה, מַכְרִיעַ אֶת כֻּלָּם:

ט אָמַר לָהֶם, צְאוּ וּרְאוּ אֵיזוֹהִי דֶרֶךְ יְשָׁרָה שֶׁיִּדְבַּק בָּהּ הָאָדָם. רַבִּי אֱלִיעֶזֶר אוֹמֵר, עַיִן טוֹבָה. רַבִּי יְהוֹשֻׁעַ אוֹמֵר, חָבֵר טוֹב. רַבִּי יוֹסֵי אוֹמֵר, שָׁכֵן טוֹב. רַבִּי שִׁמְעוֹן אוֹמֵר, הָרוֹאֶה אֶת הַנּוֹלָד. רַבִּי אֶלְעָזָר אוֹמֵר, לֵב טוֹב. אָמַר לָהֶם, רוֹאֶה אֲנִי אֶת דִּבְרֵי אֶלְעָזָר בֶּן עֲרָךְ מִדִּבְרֵיכֶם, שֶׁבִּכְלָל דְּבָרָיו דִּבְרֵיכֶם. אָמַר לָהֶם צְאוּ וּרְאוּ אֵיזוֹהִי דֶרֶךְ רָעָה שֶׁיִּתְרַחֵק מִמֶּנָּה הָאָדָם. רַבִּי אֱלִיעֶזֶר אוֹמֵר, עַיִן רָעָה. רַבִּי יְהוֹשֻׁעַ אוֹמֵר, חָבֵר רָע. רַבִּי יוֹסֵי אוֹמֵר, שָׁכֵן רָע. רַבִּי שִׁמְעוֹן אוֹמֵר, הַלֹּוֶה וְאֵינוֹ מְשַׁלֵּם. אֶחָד הַלֹּוֶה מִן הָאָדָם, כְּלֹוֶה מִן הַמָּקוֹם בָּרוּךְ הוּא, שֶׁנֶּאֱמַר (תהלים לז) לֹוֶה רָשָׁע וְלֹא יְשַׁלֵּם, וְצַדִּיק חוֹנֵן וְנוֹתֵן. רַבִּי אֶלְעָזָר אוֹמֵר, לֵב רָע. אָמַר לָהֶם, רוֹאֶה אֲנִי אֶת דִּבְרֵי אֶלְעָזָר בֶּן עֲרָךְ מִדִּבְרֵיכֶם, שֶׁבִּכְלָל דְּבָרָיו דִּבְרֵיכֶם:

י הֵם אָמְרוּ שְׁלֹשָׁה (שְׁלֹשָׁה) דְבָרִים. רַבִּי אֱלִיעֶזֶר אוֹמֵר, יְהִי כְבוֹד חֲבֵרְךָ חָבִיב עָלֶיךָ כְּשֶׁלָּךְ, וְאַל תְּהִי נוֹחַ לִכְעוֹס. וְשׁוּב יוֹם אֶחָד לִפְנֵי מִיתָתָךְ. וֶהֱוֵי מִתְחַמֵּם כְּנֶגֶד אוּרָן שֶׁל חֲכָמִים, וֶהֱוֵי זָהִיר בְּגַחַלְתָּן שֶׁלֹּא תִכָּוֶה, שֶׁנְּשִׁיכָתָן נְשִׁיכַת שׁוּעָל, וַעֲקִיצָתָן עֲקִיצַת עַקְרָב, וּלְחִישָׁתָן לְחִישַׁת שָׂרָף, וְכָל דִּבְרֵיהֶם כְּגַחֲלֵי אֵשׁ:

יא רַבִּי יְהוֹשֻׁעַ אוֹמֵר, עַיִן הָרָע, וְיֵצֶר הָרָע, וְשִׂנְאַת הַבְּרִיּוֹת, מוֹצִיאִין אֶת הָאָדָם מִן הָעוֹלָם:

יב רַבִּי יוֹסֵי אוֹמֵר, יְהִי מָמוֹן חֲבֵרְךָ חָבִיב עָלֶיךָ כְּשֶׁלָּךְ. וְהַתְקֵן עַצְמְךָ לִלְמוֹד תּוֹרָה, שֶׁאֵינָהּ יְרֻשָּׁה לָךְ. וְכָל מַעֲשֶׂיךָ יִהְיוּ לְשֵׁם שָׁמָיִם:

יג רַבִּי שִׁמְעוֹן אוֹמֵר, הֱוֵי זָהִיר בִּקְרִיאַת שְׁמַע (וּבַתְּפִלָּה). וּכְשֶׁאַתָּה מִתְפַּלֵּל, אַל תַּעַשׂ תְּפִלָּתְךָ קֶבַע, אֶלָּא רַחֲמִים וְתַחֲנוּנִים לִפְנֵי הַמָּקוֹם בָּרוּךְ הוּא, שֶׁנֶּאֱמַר (יואל ב) כִּי חַנּוּן וְרַחוּם הוּא אֶרֶךְ אַפַּיִם וְרַב חֶסֶד וְנִחָם עַל הָרָעָה. וְאַל תְּהִי רָשָׁע בִּפְנֵי עַצְמָךְ:

יד רַבִּי אֶלְעָזָר אוֹמֵר, הֱוֵי שָׁקוּד לִלְמוֹד תּוֹרָה, (וְדַע) מַה שֶׁתָּשִׁיב לָאֶפִּיקוֹרוֹס. וְדַע לִפְנֵי מִי אַתָּה עָמֵל. וְנֶאֱמָן הוּא בַּעַל מְלַאכְתְּךָ שֶׁיְּשַׁלֶּם לָךְ שְׂכַר פְּעֻלָּתָךְ:

טו רַבִּי טַרְפוֹן אוֹמֵר, הַיּוֹם קָצָר וְהַמְּלָאכָה מְרֻבָּה, וְהַפּוֹעֲלִים עֲצֵלִים, וְהַשָּׂכָר הַרְבֵּה, וּבַעַל הַבַּיִת דּוֹחֵק:

yet you are not free to avoid it. If you have studied much Torah, then you will receive much in wages for your Employer is dependable to pay the wage for your work. Know that the giving of the wages for the righteous is in the time to come."

Chapter 3

3:1 Akavya ben Mahalalel used to say, "Reflect on three things and you will not come into the grasp of sin: know where you came from; know where you are going; and [know] in whose presence you will have to make an accounting." Where do you come from? From a disgusting drop. Where are you going? To a place of dust, of worms, and of maggots. In whose presence will you have to make an accounting: the most Sovereign of sovereigns, the Holy One of Blessing.

3:2 Rabbi Chanina, the deputy of the priests, would often say, "Pray for the welfare of the government, for were it not for the fear of it, people would swallow each other alive." Rabbi Chananya ben Teradyon said, "If two sit together and exchange no words of Torah, then they are like an assembly of scoffers, for it is written, 'Nor did he sit in the assembly of the scoffers.' [Ps. 1:1] However, [when] two sit together and do exchange words of Torah, then, the Divine Presence dwells with them, even as it is written, 'Then those who feared *Adonai* spoke the one to the other, and *Adonai* listened and heard and for those who feared *Adonai* and who thought of God, a book of remembrance was inscribed.' [Mal. 3:16] This verse applies to two [people]. How may I learn from Scripture that were one person to sit and study Torah, the Holy One would grant a proper reward? From the verse that states, 'Though one sit alone and be still, yet will he receive [the reward].'" [Lam. 3:28]

3:3 Rabbi Shimon would say, "If three have eaten at one table and have not spoken words of Torah, it is as if they had eaten sacrifices offered to the dead. [Cf. Ps. 106:28.] Even Scripture says, 'All their tables are filled with filth and vomit without the Divine Presence.' [Isa. 28:8] However, three who have eaten at one table and have spoken words of Torah, Scripture states, 'He said to me, this table is in the presence of God.'" [Ezek. 41:22]

3:4 Rabbi Chanina ben Chachinai would say, "One who spends the night awake or who goes on a journey alone or who turns one's mind to useless thoughts sins against one's own soul."

3:5 Rabbi Nechunya ben Hakanah would often say, "Anyone who will accept the yoke of the Torah, from that one will be removed the yoke of the government and the yoke of worldly care. But anyone who spurns the yoke of the Torah, upon that one will be placed the yoke of the government and the yoke of worldly care."

3:6 Rabbi Chalafta ben Dosa, who lived in Kefar Chananya, used to say, "If ten sit and engage in Torah study, the

טז הוּא הָיָה אוֹמֵר, לֹא עָלֶיךָ הַמְּלָאכָה לִגְמוֹר, וְלֹא אַתָּה בֶן חוֹרִין לִבָּטֵל מִמֶּנָּה. אִם לָמַדְתָּ תּוֹרָה הַרְבֵּה, נוֹתְנִין לְךָ שָׂכָר וְנֶאֱמָן הוּא בַּעַל מְלַאכְתְּךָ שֶׁיְּשַׁלֵּם הַרְבֵּה. לְךָ שְׂכַר פְּעֻלָּתָךְ. וְדַע, מַתַּן שְׂכָרָן שֶׁל צַדִּיקִים לֶעָתִיד לָבוֹא:

פרק ג

א עֲקַבְיָא בֶן מַהֲלַלְאֵל אוֹמֵר, הִסְתַּכֵּל בִּשְׁלֹשָׁה דְבָרִים וְאֵין אַתָּה בָא לִידֵי עֲבֵרָה. דַּע, מֵאַיִן בָּאתָ, וּלְאָן אַתָּה הוֹלֵךְ, וְלִפְנֵי מִי אַתָּה עָתִיד לִתֵּן דִּין וְחֶשְׁבּוֹן. מֵאַיִן בָּאתָ, מִטִּפָּה סְרוּחָה, וּלְאָן אַתָּה הוֹלֵךְ, לִמְקוֹם עָפָר רִמָּה וְתוֹלֵעָה. וְלִפְנֵי מִי אַתָּה עָתִיד לִתֵּן דִּין וְחֶשְׁבּוֹן, לִפְנֵי מֶלֶךְ מַלְכֵי הַמְּלָכִים הַקָּדוֹשׁ בָּרוּךְ הוּא:

ב רַבִּי חֲנִינָא סְגַן הַכֹּהֲנִים אוֹמֵר, הֱוֵי מִתְפַּלֵּל בִּשְׁלוֹמָהּ שֶׁל מַלְכוּת, שֶׁאִלְמָלֵא מוֹרָאָהּ, אִישׁ אֶת רֵעֵהוּ חַיִּים בְּלָעוֹ. רַבִּי חֲנַנְיָה בֶן תְּרַדְיוֹן אוֹמֵר, שְׁנַיִם שֶׁיּוֹשְׁבִין וְאֵין בֵּינֵיהֶן דִּבְרֵי תוֹרָה, הֲרֵי זֶה מוֹשַׁב לֵצִים, שֶׁנֶּאֱמַר (תהלים א), וּבְמוֹשַׁב לֵצִים לֹא יָשָׁב. אֲבָל שְׁנַיִם שֶׁיּוֹשְׁבִין וְיֵשׁ בֵּינֵיהֶם דִּבְרֵי תוֹרָה, שְׁכִינָה שְׁרוּיָה בֵינֵיהֶם, שֶׁנֶּאֱמַר (מלאכי ג), אָז נִדְבְּרוּ יִרְאֵי יְיָ אִישׁ אֶל רֵעֵהוּ וַיַּקְשֵׁב יְיָ וַיִּשְׁמָע וַיִּכָּתֵב סֵפֶר זִכָּרוֹן לְפָנָיו לְיִרְאֵי יְיָ וּלְחֹשְׁבֵי שְׁמוֹ. אֵין לִי אֶלָּא שְׁנַיִם. מִנַּיִן שֶׁאֲפִלּוּ אֶחָד שֶׁיּוֹשֵׁב וְעוֹסֵק בַּתּוֹרָה, שֶׁהַקָּדוֹשׁ בָּרוּךְ הוּא קוֹבֵעַ לוֹ שָׂכָר, שֶׁנֶּאֱמַר (איכה ג), יֵשֵׁב בָּדָד וְיִדֹּם כִּי נָטַל עָלָיו:

ג רַבִּי שִׁמְעוֹן אוֹמֵר, שְׁלֹשָׁה שֶׁאָכְלוּ עַל שֻׁלְחָן אֶחָד וְלֹא אָמְרוּ עָלָיו דִּבְרֵי תוֹרָה, כְּאִלּוּ אָכְלוּ מִזִּבְחֵי מֵתִים, שֶׁנֶּאֱמַר (ישעיה כח), כִּי כָּל שֻׁלְחָנוֹת מָלְאוּ קִיא צֹאָה בְּלִי מָקוֹם. אֲבָל שְׁלֹשָׁה שֶׁאָכְלוּ עַל שֻׁלְחָן אֶחָד וְאָמְרוּ עָלָיו דִּבְרֵי תוֹרָה, כְּאִלּוּ אָכְלוּ מִשֻּׁלְחָנוֹ שֶׁל מָקוֹם בָּרוּךְ הוּא, שֶׁנֶּאֱמַר (יחזקאל מא), וַיְדַבֵּר אֵלַי זֶה הַשֻּׁלְחָן אֲשֶׁר לִפְנֵי ה':

ד רַבִּי חֲנִינָא בֶן חֲכִינַאי אוֹמֵר, הַנֵּעוֹר בַּלַּיְלָה וְהַמְהַלֵּךְ בַּדֶּרֶךְ יְחִידִי וְהַמְפַנֶּה לִבּוֹ לְבַטָּלָה, הֲרֵי זֶה מִתְחַיֵּב בְּנַפְשׁוֹ:

ה רַבִּי נְחוּנְיָא בֶן הַקָּנָה אוֹמֵר, כָּל הַמְקַבֵּל עָלָיו עֹל תּוֹרָה, מַעֲבִירִין מִמֶּנּוּ עֹל מַלְכוּת וְעֹל דֶּרֶךְ אֶרֶץ. וְכָל הַפּוֹרֵק מִמֶּנּוּ עֹל תּוֹרָה, נוֹתְנִין עָלָיו עֹל מַלְכוּת וְעֹל דֶּרֶךְ אֶרֶץ:

ו רַבִּי חֲלַפְתָּא בֶן דּוֹסָא אִישׁ כְּפַר חֲנַנְיָה

Divine Presence abides among them, as it is said, 'Adonai stands in the congregation of God.' [Ps. 82:1] How do we know that it applies to five? Because of the verse 'He has founded his bunch on the earth.' [Amos 9:6] How do we know that it applies even to three? Because of the verse 'He will be judged in the midst of judges.' [Ps. 82:1] How do we know that it applies even to two? The verse teaches, 'Then they who feared Adonai spoke one to the other and Adonai listened and heard.' [Mal. 3:16] It applies even to one, since it is said, 'In every place where I cause My name to be mentioned, I will come and bless you.'" [Exod. 20:24]

3:7 Rabbi Elazar who lived in Bartota would say, "Give God what is God's, since you and all that you have are God's. Thus, David said, 'Since all things come from You, that which we give You is Yours.'" [1 Chron. 29:14] Rabbi Yaakov said, "Were one to be walking on the road while studying and then stop one's studies to say, 'How beautiful is this tree!' or 'How nice is that field!' such a person would be considered by the Torah to have sinned against one's own soul."

3:8 Rabbi Dostai, the son of Rabbi Yannai, in the name of Rabbi Meir, said, "One who forgets anything one has learned, Scripture accounts it as if one had sinned against one's soul, for it says, 'Only be careful and diligently watch your soul so that you do not forget anything your eyes have seen.' [Deut. 4:9] One might think that [this caution] might apply even in the case where the studies were too difficult for the one engaged in them. Therefore, the verse continues, 'Lest they [the words of Torah] depart from your heart all the days of your life.' Thus one would sin against one's soul only if one intended to remove them from one's heart."

3:9 Rabbi Chanina ben Dosa often said, "One whose fear of sin precedes one's wisdom, one's wisdom will last. One whose wisdom precedes one's fear of sin, one's wisdom will not last." He [also] would say, "One whose deeds exceed one's wisdom, one's wisdom will last. One whose wisdom exceeds one's deeds, one's wisdom will not last."

3:10 He would often say, "Whomever people like, God likes. Whomever people do not like, God does not like." Rabbi Dosa ben Harkinas used to say, "Morning sleep, midday wine, children's talk, and attendance at the meeting places of the ignorant–all will take a person out of this world."

3:11 Rabbi Elazar of Modin used to say, "One who desecrates holy things, and one who condemns the festivals, and one who publicly shames a fellow human being, and one who breaks the covenant [Berit Milah] of Abraham our ancestor, and one who misinterprets the Torah–even if that person were to possess [great knowledge of] Torah and [were a great doer of] good deeds, that person would have no portion in the world to come."

אוֹמֵר, עֲשָׂרָה שֶׁיּוֹשְׁבִין וְעוֹסְקִין בַּתּוֹרָה, שְׁכִינָה שְׁרוּיָה בֵּינֵיהֶם, שֶׁנֶּאֱמַר (תהלים פב), אֱלֹהִים נִצָּב בַּעֲדַת אֵל.
וּמִנַּיִן אֲפִלּוּ חֲמִשָּׁה, שֶׁנֶּאֱמַר (עמוס ט), וַאֲגֻדָּתוֹ עַל אֶרֶץ יְסָדָהּ.
וּמִנַּיִן אֲפִלּוּ שְׁלֹשָׁה, שֶׁנֶּאֱמַר (תהלים פב), בְּקֶרֶב אֱלֹהִים יִשְׁפֹּט.
וּמִנַּיִן אֲפִלּוּ שְׁנַיִם, שֶׁנֶּאֱמַר (מלאכי ג), אָז נִדְבְּרוּ יִרְאֵי ה' אִישׁ אֶל רֵעֵהוּ וַיַּקְשֵׁב ה' וַיִּשְׁמָע וְגוֹ'.
וּמִנַּיִן אֲפִלּוּ אֶחָד, שֶׁנֶּאֱמַר (שמות כ), בְּכָל הַמָּקוֹם אֲשֶׁר אַזְכִּיר אֶת שְׁמִי אָבוֹא אֵלֶיךָ וּבֵרַכְתִּיךָ:

ז רַבִּי אֶלְעָזָר אִישׁ בַּרְתּוֹתָא אוֹמֵר, תֶּן לוֹ מִשֶּׁלּוֹ, שֶׁאַתָּה וְשֶׁלְּךָ שֶׁלּוֹ. וְכֵן בְּדָוִד הוּא אוֹמֵר (דברי הימים א כט) כִּי מִמְּךָ הַכֹּל וּמִיָּדְךָ נָתַנּוּ לָךְ. רַבִּי שִׁמְעוֹן אוֹמֵר, הַמְהַלֵּךְ בַּדֶּרֶךְ וְשׁוֹנֶה וּמַפְסִיק מִמִּשְׁנָתוֹ וְאוֹמֵר, מַה נָּאֶה אִילָן זֶה וּמַה נָּאֶה נִיר זֶה, מַעֲלֶה עָלָיו הַכָּתוּב כְּאִלּוּ מִתְחַיֵּב בְּנַפְשׁוֹ:

ח רַבִּי דּוֹסְתַּאי בְּרַבִּי יַנַּאי מִשּׁוּם רַבִּי מֵאִיר אוֹמֵר, כָּל הַשּׁוֹכֵחַ דָּבָר אֶחָד מִמִּשְׁנָתוֹ, מַעֲלֶה עָלָיו הַכָּתוּב כְּאִלּוּ מִתְחַיֵּב בְּנַפְשׁוֹ, שֶׁנֶּאֱמַר (דברים ד), רַק הִשָּׁמֶר לְךָ וּשְׁמֹר נַפְשְׁךָ מְאֹד פֶּן תִּשְׁכַּח אֶת הַדְּבָרִים אֲשֶׁר רָאוּ עֵינֶיךָ. יָכוֹל אֲפִלּוּ תָקְפָה עָלָיו מִשְׁנָתוֹ, תַּלְמוּד לוֹמַר (שם) וּפֶן יָסוּרוּ מִלְּבָבְךָ כֹּל יְמֵי חַיֶּיךָ, הָא אֵינוֹ מִתְחַיֵּב בְּנַפְשׁוֹ עַד שֶׁיֵּשֵׁב וִיסִירֵם מִלִּבּוֹ:

ט רַבִּי חֲנִינָא בֶּן דּוֹסָא אוֹמֵר, כָּל שֶׁיִּרְאַת חֶטְאוֹ קוֹדֶמֶת לְחָכְמָתוֹ, חָכְמָתוֹ מִתְקַיֶּמֶת.
וְכָל שֶׁחָכְמָתוֹ קוֹדֶמֶת לְיִרְאַת חֶטְאוֹ, אֵין חָכְמָתוֹ מִתְקַיֶּמֶת.
הוּא הָיָה אוֹמֵר, כָּל שֶׁמַּעֲשָׂיו מְרֻבִּין מֵחָכְמָתוֹ, חָכְמָתוֹ מִתְקַיֶּמֶת.
וְכָל שֶׁחָכְמָתוֹ מְרֻבָּה מִמַּעֲשָׂיו, אֵין חָכְמָתוֹ מִתְקַיֶּמֶת:

י הוּא הָיָה אוֹמֵר, כָּל שֶׁרוּחַ הַבְּרִיּוֹת נוֹחָה הֵימֶנּוּ, רוּחַ הַמָּקוֹם נוֹחָה הֵימֶנּוּ. וְכָל שֶׁאֵין רוּחַ הַבְּרִיּוֹת נוֹחָה הֵימֶנּוּ, אֵין רוּחַ הַמָּקוֹם נוֹחָה הֵימֶנּוּ. רַבִּי דוֹסָא בֶּן הַרְכִּינָס אוֹמֵר, שֵׁנָה שֶׁל שַׁחֲרִית, וְיַיִן שֶׁל צָהֳרַיִם, וְשִׂיחַת הַיְלָדִים, וִישִׁיבַת בָּתֵּי כְנֵסִיּוֹת שֶׁל עַמֵּי הָאָרֶץ, מוֹצִיאִין אֶת הָאָדָם מִן הָעוֹלָם:

יא רַבִּי אֶלְעָזָר הַמּוֹדָעִי אוֹמֵר, הַמְחַלֵּל אֶת הַקֳּדָשִׁים, וְהַמְבַזֶּה אֶת הַמּוֹעֲדוֹת, וְהַמַּלְבִּין פְּנֵי חֲבֵרוֹ בָרַבִּים, וְהַמֵּפֵר בְּרִיתוֹ שֶׁל אַבְרָהָם אָבִינוּ עָלָיו הַשָּׁלוֹם, וְהַמְגַלֶּה פָנִים בַּתּוֹרָה שֶׁלֹּא כַהֲלָכָה, אַף עַל פִּי שֶׁיֵּשׁ בְּיָדוֹ תוֹרָה וּמַעֲשִׂים טוֹבִים, אֵין לוֹ חֵלֶק לָעוֹלָם הַבָּא:

3:12 Rabbi Yishmael would say, "Be speedy to obey a superior; be dignified before the young; and cheerfully greet every person."

3:13 Rabbi Akiva often said, "Laughter and frivolity lead to lewdness. Tradition is a fence around the Torah. Tithes are a fence around wealth. Vows are a fence around abstinence. And silence is a fence around wisdom."

3:14 He used to say, "Human beings are loved because they were made in God's image. That they were created in God's image was made known by a special love, as it is said, 'For God made human beings in the divine image.' [Gen. 9:6] Israel is loved for they are called children of God. That they were called children of God was made known to them by a special love, as it is said, 'You are children of *Adonai* your God.' [Deut. 14:1] Israel is [even more] loved because to them was given a precious instrument. That such a precious instrument was given to them was made known to them by a special love, as it is said, 'For I have given you a good doctrine, do not forsake my Torah.'" [Prov. 4:2]

3:15 All is foreseen, yet [free] choice is given. By [God's] goodness is the world judged. Yet all things follow the larger portion of [human] acts.

3:16 He used to say, "Everything is given on pledge and a net is spread out for all that lives. The shop is open; the shopkeeper extends credit; the ledger is open; and the hand writes. One may come and borrow, but the collectors make their rounds each and every day; and they collect whether one wants it or not; what they have got, they can depend on, for the judgment is a true one, and everything is prepared for the banquet."

3:17 Rabbi Elazar ben Azaryah said, "Where there is no Torah, there will be no good conduct; where there is no good conduct, there will be no Torah. Where there is no wisdom, there will be no reverence; where there is no reverence, there will be no wisdom. Where there is no understanding, there will be no knowledge; where there is no knowledge, there will be no understanding. Where there is no bread [literally, flour], there will be no Torah; where there is no Torah, there will be no bread." He would often say, "To what shall be compared one whose wisdom is greater than one's deeds? To a tree whose branches are many, but whose roots are few, so that, when the wind comes, it will uproot it and overturn it, as it says, 'One shall be like a tamerisk in the desert and shall not see when good comes; but shall inhabit the parched places in the wilderness.' [Jer. 17:6] To what shall be compared one whose works are more numerous than one's wisdom? To a tree whose branches are few, but whose roots are many, so that, even if all the winds of the world were to come and blow upon it, they could not move it from its place, even as it says, 'For one shall be as a tree planted by the water, that spreads out its roots by the river. It shall not fear when heat comes, for its leaf shall be green. It shall not worry in a year of drought, for it shall never cease yielding fruit.'" [Jer. 17:8]

יב רַבִּי יִשְׁמָעֵאל אוֹמֵר, הֱוֵי קַל לָרֹאשׁ וְנוֹחַ לַתִּשְׁחֹרֶת, וֶהֱוֵי מְקַבֵּל אֶת כָּל הָאָדָם בְּשִׂמְחָה:

יג רַבִּי עֲקִיבָא אוֹמֵר, שְׂחוֹק וְקַלּוּת רֹאשׁ מַרְגִּילִין לְעֶרְוָה. מָסוֹרֶת סְיָג לַתּוֹרָה. מַעַשְׂרוֹת, סְיָג לָעשֶׁר. נְדָרִים, סְיָג לַפְּרִישׁוּת. סְיָג לַחָכְמָה, שְׁתִיקָה:

יד הוּא הָיָה אוֹמֵר, חָבִיב אָדָם שֶׁנִּבְרָא בְצֶלֶם. חִבָּה יְתֵרָה נוֹדַעַת לוֹ שֶׁנִּבְרָא בְצֶלֶם, שֶׁנֶּאֱמַר (בראשית ט), כִּי בְּצֶלֶם אֱלֹהִים עָשָׂה אֶת הָאָדָם. חֲבִיבִין יִשְׂרָאֵל שֶׁנִּקְרְאוּ בָנִים לַמָּקוֹם. חִבָּה יְתֵרָה נוֹדַעַת לָהֶם שֶׁנִּקְרְאוּ בָנִים לַמָּקוֹם, שֶׁנֶּאֱמַר (דברים יד), בָּנִים אַתֶּם לַה' אֱלֹהֵיכֶם. חֲבִיבִין יִשְׂרָאֵל, שֶׁנִּתַּן לָהֶם כְּלִי חֶמְדָּה. חִבָּה יְתֵרָה נוֹדַעַת לָהֶם שֶׁנִּתַּן לָהֶם כְּלִי חֶמְדָּה שֶׁבּוֹ נִבְרָא הָעוֹלָם, שֶׁנֶּאֱמַר (משלי ד), כִּי לֶקַח טוֹב נָתַתִּי לָכֶם, תּוֹרָתִי אַל תַּעֲזֹבוּ:

טו הַכֹּל צָפוּי, וְהָרְשׁוּת נְתוּנָה, וּבְטוֹב הָעוֹלָם נִדּוֹן. וְהַכֹּל לְפִי רֹב הַמַּעֲשֶׂה:

טז הוּא הָיָה אוֹמֵר, הַכֹּל נָתוּן בָּעֵרָבוֹן, וּמְצוּדָה פְרוּסָה עַל כָּל הַחַיִּים. הַחֲנוּת פְּתוּחָה, וְהַחֶנְוָנִי מַקִּיף, וְהַפִּנְקָס פָּתוּחַ, וְהַיָּד כּוֹתֶבֶת, וְכָל הָרוֹצֶה לִלְווֹת יָבוֹא וְיִלְוֶה, וְהַגַּבָּאִים מַחֲזִירִים תָּדִיר בְּכָל יוֹם, וְנִפְרָעִין מִן הָאָדָם מִדַּעְתּוֹ וְשֶׁלֹּא מִדַּעְתּוֹ, וְיֵשׁ לָהֶם עַל מַה שֶׁיִּסְמֹכוּ, וְהַדִּין דִּין אֱמֶת, וְהַכֹּל מְתֻקָּן לַסְּעוּדָה:

יז רַבִּי אֶלְעָזָר בֶּן עֲזַרְיָה אוֹמֵר, אִם אֵין תּוֹרָה, אֵין דֶּרֶךְ אֶרֶץ. אִם אֵין דֶּרֶךְ אֶרֶץ, אֵין תּוֹרָה. אִם אֵין חָכְמָה, אֵין יִרְאָה. אִם אֵין יִרְאָה, אֵין חָכְמָה. אִם אֵין בִּינָה, אֵין דָּעַת. אִם אֵין דַּעַת, אֵין בִּינָה. אִם אֵין קֶמַח, אֵין תּוֹרָה. אִם אֵין תּוֹרָה, אֵין קֶמַח. הוּא הָיָה אוֹמֵר, כָּל שֶׁחָכְמָתוֹ מְרֻבָּה מִמַּעֲשָׂיו, לְמָה הוּא דוֹמֶה, לְאִילָן שֶׁעֲנָפָיו מְרֻבִּין וְשָׁרָשָׁיו מֻעָטִין, וְהָרוּחַ בָּאָה וְעוֹקַרְתּוּ וְהוֹפַכְתּוּ עַל פָּנָיו, שֶׁנֶּאֱמַר (ירמיה יז), וְהָיָה כְּעַרְעָר בָּעֲרָבָה וְלֹא יִרְאֶה כִּי יָבוֹא טוֹב וְשָׁכַן חֲרֵרִים בַּמִּדְבָּר אֶרֶץ מְלֵחָה וְלֹא תֵשֵׁב. אֲבָל כָּל שֶׁמַּעֲשָׂיו מְרֻבִּין מֵחָכְמָתוֹ, לְמָה הוּא דוֹמֶה, לְאִילָן שֶׁעֲנָפָיו מֻעָטִין וְשָׁרָשָׁיו מְרֻבִּין, שֶׁאֲפִלּוּ כָּל הָרוּחוֹת שֶׁבָּעוֹלָם בָּאוֹת וְנוֹשְׁבוֹת בּוֹ אֵין מְזִיזִין אוֹתוֹ מִמְּקוֹמוֹ, שֶׁנֶּאֱמַר (שם), וְהָיָה כְּעֵץ שָׁתוּל עַל מַיִם וְעַל יוּבַל יְשַׁלַּח שָׁרָשָׁיו וְלֹא יִרְאֶה כִּי יָבֹא חֹם, וְהָיָה עָלֵהוּ רַעֲנָן, וּבִשְׁנַת בַּצֹּרֶת לֹא יִדְאָג, וְלֹא יָמִישׁ מֵעֲשׂוֹת פֶּרִי:

3:18 Rabbi Elazar ben Chisma would say, "[Laws concerning] the offering of birds and the onset of menstruation are the main elements of the laws, while astronomy and geometry are but the appetizers of wisdom."

Chapter 4

4:1 Ben Zoma said, "Who is wise? The one who learns from everyone, as it is said, 'From all who would teach me, have I gained understanding.' [Ps. 119:99] Who is mighty? One who controls one's [natural] urges, as it is said, 'One who is slow to anger is better than the mighty and one who rules one's spirit than one who conquers a city.' [Prov. 16:32] Who is rich? One who is happy with what one has, as it says, 'When you eat what your hands have provided, you shall be happy and good will be yours.' [Ps. 128:2] You shall be happy in this world; and good will be yours in the world to come. Who is honored? One who honors others, as it says, 'Those who honor Me, will I honor, and those who despise Me will be lightly esteemed.'" [1 Sam. 2:30]

4:2 Ben Azzai would say, "Run to do the least of the commandments as you would to do the most important. Run away from a transgression, for a commandment pulls along a commandment and a transgression pulls along a transgression. The reward of a commandment is a commandment and the reward of a transgression is a transgression."

4:3 He used to say, "Treat no one lightly and think nothing is useless, for everyone has one's moment and everything has its place."

4:4 Rabbi Levitas, a man of Yavneh, used to say, "Be exceedingly humble of spirit, for the human hope is only the worm." Rabbi Yochanan ben Beroka would say, "Whoever would profane the name of God in secret will be punished in public. It makes no difference whether such profanation was intended or not."

4:5 Rabbi Yishmael, his son, was accustomed to saying, "The one who studies in order to teach will be enabled to study and to teach. The one who studies in order to practice will be enabled to study and to teach, to observe and to practice." Rabbi Tzadok said, "Do not separate yourself from the community. Don't be like those who try to influence judges. Don't use [the words of the Torah] as a crown to build yourself up, nor as an adze to dig with, as Hillel said, 'The one who would make use of the crown [of the Torah] will pass away.' Thus you may learn that whoever [improperly] uses the word of Torah takes one's own life from this world."

4:6 Rabbi Yose used to say, "Whoever honors the Torah will be honored by others. Whoever dishonors the Torah will be dishonored by others."

4:7 Rabbi Yishmael, his son, would say, "Whoever restrains oneself from acting as judge removes from oneself enmity,

יח רַבִּי אֶלְעָזָר בֶּן חִסְמָא אוֹמֵר, קִנִּין וּפִתְחֵי נִדָּה, הֵן הֵן גּוּפֵי הֲלָכוֹת. תְּקוּפוֹת וְגִמַטְרִיָּאוֹת, פַּרְפְּרָאוֹת לַחָכְמָה:

פרק ד

א בֶּן זוֹמָא אוֹמֵר, אֵיזֶהוּ חָכָם, הַלּוֹמֵד מִכָּל אָדָם, שֶׁנֶּאֱמַר (תהלים קיט), מִכָּל מְלַמְּדַי הִשְׂכַּלְתִּי כִּי עֵדְוֹתֶיךָ שִׂיחָה לִי. אֵיזֶהוּ גִבּוֹר, הַכּוֹבֵשׁ אֶת יִצְרוֹ, שֶׁנֶּאֱמַר (משלי טז), טוֹב אֶרֶךְ אַפַּיִם מִגִּבּוֹר וּמֹשֵׁל בְּרוּחוֹ מִלֹּכֵד עִיר. אֵיזֶהוּ עָשִׁיר הַשָּׂמֵחַ בְּחֶלְקוֹ, שֶׁנֶּאֱמַר (תהלים קכח), יְגִיעַ כַּפֶּיךָ כִּי תֹאכֵל אַשְׁרֶיךָ וְטוֹב לָךְ. אַשְׁרֶיךָ, בָּעוֹלָם הַזֶּה. וְטוֹב לָךְ, לָעוֹלָם הַבָּא. אֵיזֶהוּ מְכֻבָּד, הַמְכַבֵּד אֶת הַבְּרִיּוֹת, שֶׁנֶּאֱמַר (שמואל א ב), כִּי מְכַבְּדַי אֲכַבֵּד וּבֹזַי יֵקָלּוּ:

ב בֶּן עַזַּאי אוֹמֵר, הֱוֵי רָץ לְמִצְוָה קַלָּה (כְּבַחֲמוּרָה), וּבוֹרֵחַ מִן הָעֲבֵרָה. שֶׁמִּצְוָה גוֹרֶרֶת מִצְוָה, וַעֲבֵרָה גוֹרֶרֶת עֲבֵרָה. שֶׁשְּׂכַר מִצְוָה, מִצְוָה. וּשְׂכַר עֲבֵרָה, עֲבֵרָה:

ג הוּא הָיָה אוֹמֵר, אַל תְּהִי בָז לְכָל אָדָם, וְאַל תְּהִי מַפְלִיג לְכָל דָּבָר, שֶׁאֵין לְךָ אָדָם שֶׁאֵין לוֹ שָׁעָה וְאֵין לְךָ דָבָר שֶׁאֵין לוֹ מָקוֹם:

ד רַבִּי לְוִיטָס אִישׁ יַבְנֶה אוֹמֵר, מְאֹד מְאֹד הֱוֵי שְׁפַל רוּחַ, שֶׁתִּקְוַת אֱנוֹשׁ רִמָּה. רַבִּי יוֹחָנָן בֶּן בְּרוֹקָא אוֹמֵר, כָּל הַמְחַלֵּל שֵׁם שָׁמַיִם בַּסֵּתֶר, נִפְרָעִין מִמֶּנּוּ בַּגָּלוּי. אֶחָד שׁוֹגֵג וְאֶחָד מֵזִיד בְּחִלּוּל הַשֵּׁם:

ה רַבִּי יִשְׁמָעֵאל (בְּנוֹ) אוֹמֵר, הַלּוֹמֵד תּוֹרָה עַל מְנָת לְלַמֵּד, מַסְפִּיקִין בְּיָדוֹ לִלְמוֹד וּלְלַמֵּד. וְהַלּוֹמֵד עַל מְנָת לַעֲשׂוֹת, מַסְפִּיקִין בְּיָדוֹ לִלְמוֹד וּלְלַמֵּד לִשְׁמוֹר וְלַעֲשׂוֹת. רַבִּי צָדוֹק אוֹמֵר, אַל תַּעֲשֵׂם עֲטָרָה לְהִתְגַּדֵּל בָּהֶם, וְלֹא קַרְדֹּם לַחְפּוֹר בָּהֶם. וְכָךְ הָיָה הִלֵּל אוֹמֵר, וּדְאִשְׁתַּמֵּשׁ בְּתַגָּא, חֲלָף. הָא לָמַדְתָּ, כָּל הַנֶּהֱנֶה מִדִּבְרֵי תוֹרָה, נוֹטֵל חַיָּיו מִן הָעוֹלָם:

ו רַבִּי יוֹסֵי אוֹמֵר, כָּל הַמְכַבֵּד אֶת הַתּוֹרָה, גּוּפוֹ מְכֻבָּד עַל הַבְּרִיּוֹת. וְכָל הַמְחַלֵּל אֶת הַתּוֹרָה, גּוּפוֹ מְחֻלָּל עַל הַבְּרִיּוֹת:

ז רַבִּי יִשְׁמָעֵאל בְּנוֹ אוֹמֵר, הַחוֹשֵׂךְ עַצְמוֹ מִן הַדִּין, פּוֹרֵק מִמֶּנּוּ אֵיבָה וְגָזֵל וּשְׁבוּעַת שָׁוְא.

robbery, and perjury. Whoever pompously renders decisions is a wicked and arrogant fool."

4:8 He used to say, "Don't judge alone, for only the One [God] may do so. Don't say [to your fellow judges], 'Accept my view,' for it is up to them [to make that decision] and not up to you."

4:9 Rabbi Yonatan would say, "Whoever may fulfill the Torah when poor will in the end fulfill it when rich. Whoever may neglect the Torah when rich will in the end neglect the Torah when poor."

4:10 Rabbi Meir would say, "Do less business and do more Torah. Be humble in everyone's presence. If you have neglected the Torah, there are many who are like you. If you have labored in the Torah, God will give you a great reward."

4:11 Rabbi Eliezer ben Yaakov would say, "Whoever fulfills one commandment has acquired one advocate while whoever has committed one transgression has acquired one accuser. Repentance and good deeds may serve as a shield against punishment." Rabbi Yochanan Ha-Sandelar used to say, "Any gathering for the sake of Heaven will have permanence but that which is not for the sake of Heaven will not."

4:12 Rabbi Elazar ben Shammua would say, "Let the honor of your student be as dear to you as your own. Let the honor of your associate be equal to the respect due to your teacher. Let the respect due to your teacher be equivalent to the reverence due to Heaven."

4:13 Rabbi Yehudah used to say, "Be very careful in [your] study for a mistake [by a scholar] will be considered as a deliberate sin." Rabbi Shimon said, "There are three crowns: the crown of Torah; the crown of priesthood; and the crown of royalty. However, the crown of a good name is greater than all of them."

4:14 Rabbi Nehorai said, "Leave home and go to a place of Torah. Don't say that Torah will come to you or that your companions will make it yours. Don't depend on your own understanding."

4:15 Rabbi Yannai said, "[The reason] why the guilty prosper or the innocent suffer is not within our grasp." Rabbi Matya ben Charash said, "Be the first to greet everyone; be a tail to lions rather than a head to foxes."

4:16 Rabbi Yaakov said, "This world is like a foyer before the world to come. Prepare yourself in the foyer so that you will be able to enter the banquet hall."

4:17 He would often say, "An hour spent in penitence and good deeds in this world is better than all of life in the world to come. An hour of contentment in the world to come is better than all of life in this world."

וְהַגַּס לִבּוֹ בַהוֹרָאָה, שׁוֹטֶה רָשָׁע וְגַס רוּחַ:

ח הוּא הָיָה אוֹמֵר, אַל תְּהִי דָן יְחִידִי, שֶׁאֵין דָּן יְחִידִי אֶלָּא אֶחָד. וְאַל תֹּאמַר קַבְּלוּ דַעְתִּי, שֶׁהֵן רַשָּׁאִין וְלֹא אָתָּה:

ט רַבִּי יוֹנָתָן אוֹמֵר, כָּל הַמְקַיֵּם אֶת הַתּוֹרָה מֵעֹנִי, סוֹפוֹ לְקַיְּמָהּ מֵעֹשֶׁר. וְכָל הַמְבַטֵּל אֶת הַתּוֹרָה מֵעֹשֶׁר, סוֹפוֹ לְבַטְּלָהּ מֵעֹנִי:

י רַבִּי מֵאִיר אוֹמֵר, הֱוֵי מְמַעֵט בָּעֵסֶק, וַעֲסוֹק בַּתּוֹרָה. וֶהֱוֵי שְׁפַל רוּחַ בִּפְנֵי כָל אָדָם. וְאִם בָּטַלְתָּ מִן הַתּוֹרָה, יֶשׁ לְךָ בְטֵלִים הַרְבֵּה כְּנֶגְדָּךְ. וְאִם עָמַלְתָּ בַּתּוֹרָה, יֶשׁ לוֹ שָׂכָר הַרְבֵּה לִתֶּן לָךְ:

יא רַבִּי אֱלִיעֶזֶר בֶּן יַעֲקֹב אוֹמֵר, הָעוֹשֶׂה מִצְוָה אַחַת, קוֹנֶה לוֹ פְרַקְלִיט אֶחָד. וְהָעוֹבֵר עֲבֵרָה אַחַת, קוֹנֶה לוֹ קַטֵּיגוֹר אֶחָד. תְּשׁוּבָה וּמַעֲשִׂים טוֹבִים, כִּתְרִיס בִּפְנֵי הַפֻּרְעָנוּת. רַבִּי יוֹחָנָן הַסַּנְדְּלָר אוֹמֵר, כָּל כְּנֵסִיָּה שֶׁהִיא לְשֵׁם שָׁמַיִם, סוֹפָהּ לְהִתְקַיֵּם. וְשֶׁאֵינָהּ לְשֵׁם שָׁמַיִם, אֵין סוֹפָהּ לְהִתְקַיֵּם:

יב רַבִּי אֶלְעָזָר בֶּן שַׁמּוּעַ אוֹמֵר, יְהִי כְבוֹד תַּלְמִידְךָ חָבִיב עָלֶיךָ כְּשֶׁלָּךְ, וּכְבוֹד חֲבֵרְךָ כְּמוֹרָא רַבָּךְ, וּמוֹרָא רַבָּךְ כְּמוֹרָא שָׁמָיִם:

יג רַבִּי יְהוּדָה אוֹמֵר, הֱוֵי זָהִיר בַּתַּלְמוּד, שֶׁשִּׁגְגַת תַּלְמוּד עוֹלָה זָדוֹן. רַבִּי שִׁמְעוֹן אוֹמֵר, שְׁלֹשָׁה כְתָרִים הֵם, כֶּתֶר תּוֹרָה וְכֶתֶר כְּהֻנָּה וְכֶתֶר מַלְכוּת, וְכֶתֶר שֵׁם טוֹב עוֹלֶה עַל גַּבֵּיהֶן:

יד רַבִּי נְהוֹרַאי אוֹמֵר, הֱוֵי גוֹלֶה לִמְקוֹם תּוֹרָה וְאַל תֹּאמַר שֶׁהִיא תָבוֹא אַחֲרֶיךָ, שֶׁחֲבֵרֶיךָ יְקַיְּמוּהָ בְיָדֶךָ. וְאֶל בִּינָתְךָ אַל תִּשָּׁעֵן:

טו רַבִּי יַנַּאי אוֹמֵר, אֵין בְּיָדֵינוּ לֹא מִשַּׁלְוַת הָרְשָׁעִים וְאַף לֹא מִיִּסּוּרֵי הַצַּדִּיקִים. רַבִּי מַתְיָא בֶּן חָרָשׁ אוֹמֵר, הֱוֵי מַקְדִּים בִּשְׁלוֹם כָּל אָדָם. וֶהֱוֵי זָנָב לָאֲרָיוֹת, וְאַל תְּהִי רֹאשׁ לַשּׁוּעָלִים:

טז רַבִּי יַעֲקֹב אוֹמֵר, הָעוֹלָם הַזֶּה דּוֹמֶה לִפְרוֹזְדוֹר בִּפְנֵי הָעוֹלָם הַבָּא. הַתְקֵן עַצְמְךָ בַפְּרוֹזְדוֹר, כְּדֵי שֶׁתִּכָּנֵס לַטְּרַקְלִין:

יז הוּא הָיָה אוֹמֵר, יָפָה שָׁעָה אַחַת בִּתְשׁוּבָה וּמַעֲשִׂים טוֹבִים בָּעוֹלָם הַזֶּה, מִכָּל חַיֵּי הָעוֹלָם הַבָּא. וְיָפָה שָׁעָה אַחַת שֶׁל קוֹרַת רוּחַ בָּעוֹלָם הַבָּא, מִכָּל חַיֵּי הָעוֹלָם הַזֶּה:

4:18 Rabbi Shimon ben Elazar said, "When your friend becomes angry, don't try to calm him. When he is recently bereaved, don't try to comfort him. When he is about to make an oath, don't ask him questions. Just after he has been disgraced, don't try to see him."

4:19 Shmuel Ha-Katan said, "Rejoice not when your enemy falls. Let not your heart be glad when another stumbles. *Adonai* may see it, and [if] it displeases God, God may remove from him [the enemy] divine wrath." [Prov. 24:17, 18]

4:20 Elisha ben Abuyah said, "Regarding the one who studies when young, to what can that person be compared? To ink written on new paper. Regarding the one who studies when old, to what can that person be compared? To ink written on paper that has been erased." Rabbi Yose ben Yehudah of Kefar Ha-Bavli said, "Regarding the one who learns from the young, to what can this person be compared? To one eating unripe grapes and drinking wine from the wine-press. Regarding the person who learns from the old, to what can this person be compared? To one eating ripe grapes and drinking old wine." Rabbi [however] said, "Don't look at the wine flask, but rather at what is in it. For there are new wine flasks filled with old wine, and there are old wine flasks that don't have even new wine."

4:21 Rabbi Elazar Ha-Kappar said, "Envy, lust, and [the pursuit of] glory take a person out of this world."

4:22 He used to say, "Those who are born will die. Those who die will live again. Those who [then] live are to be judged, to know, to make known, and to let it be known who is God, who is the Maker, who is the Creator, who is the One who understands, who is the Judge, who is the Witness, who is the Litigant. The Holy One of Blessing is the one who will judge [a judge] without iniquity, without forgetfulness, without partiality, without being bribed. Know that everything will be added up. Don't let your inclination [to do evil] persuade you that you will be able to escape in the grave, for against your will were you formed. Against your will were you born. Against your will you live. Against your will you will die. Against your will you will make a reckoning before the Ruler of rulers, the Holy One of Blessing."

Chapter 5

5:1 The world was created by ten statements. Why does the Torah teach [us] that? Indeed, the world could have been created by one statement! That teaching was [offered] to punish the wicked who would destroy the world that was created by ten statements and to reward the righteous who maintain the world created by [these] ten statements.

5:2 There were ten generations from Adam to Noah to prove the patience of God. Although all those generations provoked God, only then [after ten generations] did God bring the Flood upon them. There were ten generations

יח רַבִּי שִׁמְעוֹן בֶּן אֶלְעָזָר אוֹמֵר, אַל תְּרַצֶּה אֶת חֲבֵרְךָ בִּשְׁעַת כַּעֲסוֹ, וְאַל תְּנַחֲמֶנּוּ בְּשָׁעָה שֶׁמֵּתוֹ מֻטָּל לְפָנָיו, וְאַל תִּשְׁאַל לוֹ בִּשְׁעַת נִדְרוֹ, וְאַל תִּשְׁתַּדֵּל לִרְאוֹתוֹ בִּשְׁעַת קַלְקָלָתוֹ:

יט שְׁמוּאֵל הַקָּטָן אוֹמֵר, (משלי כד) בִּנְפֹל אוֹיְבִךָ אַל תִּשְׂמָח וּבִכָּשְׁלוֹ אַל יָגֵל לִבֶּךָ, פֶּן יִרְאֶה יְיָ וְרַע בְּעֵינָיו וְהֵשִׁיב מֵעָלָיו אַפּוֹ:

כ אֱלִישָׁע בֶּן אֲבוּיָה אוֹמֵר, הַלוֹמֵד יֶלֶד לְמָה הוּא דוֹמֶה, לִדְיוֹ כְתוּבָה עַל נְיָר חָדָשׁ. וְהַלוֹמֵד זָקֵן לְמָה הוּא דוֹמֶה, לִדְיוֹ כְתוּבָה עַל נְיָר מָחוּק. רַבִּי יוֹסֵי בַר יְהוּדָה אִישׁ כְּפַר הַבַּבְלִי אוֹמֵר, הַלוֹמֵד מִן הַקְּטַנִּים לְמָה הוּא דוֹמֶה, לְאוֹכֵל עֲנָבִים קֵהוֹת וְשׁוֹתֶה יַיִן מִגִּתּוֹ. וְהַלוֹמֵד מִן הַזְּקֵנִים לְמָה הוּא דוֹמֶה, לְאוֹכֵל עֲנָבִים בְּשׁוּלוֹת וְשׁוֹתֶה יַיִן יָשָׁן. רַבִּי אוֹמֵר, אַל תִּסְתַּכֵּל בַּקַּנְקַן, אֶלָּא בַּמֶּה שֶׁיֶּשׁ בּוֹ. יֵשׁ קַנְקַן חָדָשׁ מָלֵא יָשָׁן, וְיָשָׁן שֶׁאֲפִלּוּ חָדָשׁ אֵין בּוֹ:

כא רַבִּי אֶלְעָזָר הַקַּפָּר אוֹמֵר, הַקִּנְאָה וְהַתַּאֲוָה וְהַכָּבוֹד מוֹצִיאִין אֶת הָאָדָם מִן הָעוֹלָם:

כב הוּא הָיָה אוֹמֵר, הַיִּלּוֹדִים לָמוּת, וְהַמֵּתִים לְהַחֲיוֹת, וְהַחַיִּים לָדוֹן. לֵידַע לְהוֹדִיעַ וּלְהִוָּדַע שֶׁהוּא אֵל, הוּא הַיּוֹצֵר, הוּא הַבּוֹרֵא, הוּא הַמֵּבִין, הוּא הַדַּיָּן, הוּא עֵד, הוּא בַּעַל דִּין, וְהוּא עָתִיד לָדוֹן. בָּרוּךְ הוּא, שֶׁאֵין לְפָנָיו לֹא עַוְלָה וְלֹא שִׁכְחָה וְלֹא מַשּׂוֹא פָנִים וְלֹא מִקַּח שׁוֹחַד, שֶׁהַכֹּל שֶׁלּוֹ. וְדַע שֶׁהַכֹּל לְפִי הַחֶשְׁבּוֹן. וְאַל יַבְטִיחֲךָ יִצְרֶךָ שֶׁהַשְּׁאוֹל בֵּית מָנוֹס לָךְ, שֶׁעַל כָּרְחֲךָ אַתָּה נוֹצָר, וְעַל כָּרְחֲךָ אַתָּה נוֹלָד, וְעַל כָּרְחֲךָ אַתָּה חַי, וְעַל כָּרְחֲךָ אַתָּה מֵת, וְעַל כָּרְחֲךָ אַתָּה עָתִיד לִתֵּן דִּין וְחֶשְׁבּוֹן לִפְנֵי מֶלֶךְ מַלְכֵי הַמְּלָכִים הַקָּדוֹשׁ בָּרוּךְ הוּא:

פרק ה

א בַּעֲשָׂרָה מַאֲמָרוֹת נִבְרָא הָעוֹלָם. וּמַה תַּלְמוּד לוֹמַר, וַהֲלֹא בְמַאֲמָר אֶחָד יָכוֹל לְהִבָּרְאוֹת, אֶלָּא לְהִפָּרַע מִן הָרְשָׁעִים שֶׁמְּאַבְּדִין אֶת הָעוֹלָם שֶׁנִּבְרָא בַּעֲשָׂרָה מַאֲמָרוֹת, וְלִתֵּן שָׂכָר טוֹב לַצַּדִּיקִים שֶׁמְּקַיְּמִין אֶת הָעוֹלָם שֶׁנִּבְרָא בַּעֲשָׂרָה מַאֲמָרוֹת:

ב עֲשָׂרָה דוֹרוֹת מֵאָדָם וְעַד נֹחַ, לְהוֹדִיעַ כַּמָּה אֶרֶךְ אַפַּיִם לְפָנָיו, שֶׁכָּל הַדּוֹרוֹת הָיוּ מַכְעִיסִין וּבָאִין עַד שֶׁהֵבִיא עֲלֵיהֶם אֶת מֵי הַמַּבּוּל. עֲשָׂרָה דוֹרוֹת מִנֹּחַ וְעַד אַבְרָהָם,

from Noah to Abraham to prove the patience of God. Although all those generations provoked God, only then [after ten generations] did Abraham come to receive the reward [that might have been intended] for all of them.

5:3 Abraham was tested ten times. He withstood every test to show [how] great was his love [for God].

5:4 Ten miracles were performed for our ancestors in Egypt. Ten occurred at the sea. Ten plagues were brought by the Holy One of Blessing against the Egyptians in Egypt and ten at the sea. Ten times did our ancestors test the Holy One of Blessing, as it says, "And they tested Me these ten times and would not hearken to My voice." [Num. 14:22]

5:5 Ten miracles were performed for our ancestors in the Temple. The odor of the meat of the sacrifice never caused a woman to miscarry. That meat never became putrid. No fly was ever seen in the slaughterhouse. No [disqualifying] pollution ever befell the High Priest on the Day of Atonement. Rain never put out the fire of the wood arranged [on the altar]. The wind did not disturb the smoke column [from the altar]. No defect was ever found in the *omer,* or in the two loaves, or in the showbread. Although the people were tightly pressed together, there was plenty of room when they prostrated themselves. No one was ever hurt by snake or scorpion in Jerusalem. No one ever said, "There is no room for me to spend the night in Jerusalem."

5:6 Ten things were created on the eve of the [first] Shabbat at twilight. They are: the mouth of the earth; the mouth of the well; the mouth of the ass; the rainbow; the manna; the staff [of Moses]; the *shamir;* the writing; the writing instrument; and the tablets. Some say: destructive spirits; the grave of Moses; and the ram of our patriarch Abraham. Some even say the first tongs [which are] made by tongs.

5:7 Seven things distinguish a fool and seven things distinguish a wise person. The wise person does not speak in the presence of one who is wiser. The wise person does not interrupt when another is speaking. The wise person is not in a hurry to answer. The wise person asks according to the subject and answers according to the Law. The wise person speaks about the first matter first and the last matter last. If there is something the wise person has not heard [and therefore does not know], the wise person says, "I have never heard [of it]." The wise person acknowledges what is true. The opposite of all these qualities is found in a fool.

5:8 Seven kinds of punishment come into the world for seven categories of transgression. If some give tithes while some do not, a famine resulting from drought ensues. Thus, some will be sated, and others will starve. If all have decided not to tithe, then a famine resulting from anxiety and drought ensues. If all resolve not to give the *challah,* then a totally destructive famine will ensue. Pestilence comes to the world because of crimes that the Torah declares deserving of death but that could not be judged by

לְהוֹדִיעַ כַּמָּה אֶרֶךְ אַפַּיִם לְפָנָיו, שֶׁכָּל הַדּוֹרוֹת הָיוּ מַכְעִיסִין וּבָאִין, עַד שֶׁבָּא אַבְרָהָם וְקִבֵּל (עָלָיו) שְׂכַר כֻּלָּם:

ג עֲשָׂרָה נִסְיוֹנוֹת נִתְנַסָּה אַבְרָהָם אָבִינוּ עָלָיו הַשָּׁלוֹם וְעָמַד בְּכֻלָּם, לְהוֹדִיעַ כַּמָּה חִבָּתוֹ שֶׁל אַבְרָהָם אָבִינוּ:

ד עֲשָׂרָה נִסִּים נַעֲשׂוּ לַאֲבוֹתֵינוּ בְמִצְרַיִם וַעֲשָׂרָה עַל הַיָּם. עֶשֶׂר מַכּוֹת הֵבִיא הַקָּדוֹשׁ בָּרוּךְ הוּא עַל הַמִּצְרִיִּים בְּמִצְרַיִם וְעֶשֶׂר עַל הַיָּם. עֲשָׂרָה נִסְיוֹנוֹת נִסּוּ אֲבוֹתֵינוּ אֶת הַקָּדוֹשׁ בָּרוּךְ הוּא בַמִּדְבָּר, שֶׁנֶּאֱמַר, וַיְנַסּוּ אֹתִי זֶה עֶשֶׂר פְּעָמִים וְלֹא שָׁמְעוּ בְּקוֹלִי:

ה עֲשָׂרָה נִסִּים נַעֲשׂוּ לַאֲבוֹתֵינוּ בְּבֵית הַמִּקְדָּשׁ. לֹא הִפִּילָה אִשָּׁה מֵרֵיחַ בְּשַׂר הַקֹּדֶשׁ, וְלֹא הִסְרִיחַ בְּשַׂר הַקֹּדֶשׁ מֵעוֹלָם, וְלֹא נִרְאָה זְבוּב בְּבֵית הַמִּטְבָּחַיִם, וְלֹא אֵרַע קֶרִי לְכֹהֵן גָּדוֹל בְּיוֹם הַכִּפּוּרִים, וְלֹא כִבּוּ גְשָׁמִים אֵשׁ שֶׁל עֲצֵי הַמַּעֲרָכָה, וְלֹא נָצְחָה הָרוּחַ אֶת עַמּוּד הֶעָשָׁן, וְלֹא נִמְצָא פְסוּל בָּעֹמֶר וּבִשְׁתֵּי הַלֶּחֶם וּבְלֶחֶם הַפָּנִים, עוֹמְדִים צְפוּפִים וּמִשְׁתַּחֲוִים רְוָחִים, וְלֹא הִזִּיק נָחָשׁ וְעַקְרָב בִּירוּשָׁלַיִם מֵעוֹלָם, וְלֹא אָמַר אָדָם לַחֲבֵרוֹ צַר לִי הַמָּקוֹם שֶׁאָלִין בִּירוּשָׁלָיִם:

ו עֲשָׂרָה דְבָרִים נִבְרְאוּ בְּעֶרֶב שַׁבָּת בֵּין הַשְּׁמָשׁוֹת, וְאֵלּוּ הֵן, פִּי הָאָרֶץ, וּפִי הַבְּאֵר, וּפִי הָאָתוֹן, וְהַקֶּשֶׁת, וְהַמָּן, וְהַמַּטֶּה, וְהַשָּׁמִיר, וְהַכְּתָב, וְהַמִּכְתָּב, וְהַלּוּחוֹת. וְיֵשׁ אוֹמְרִים, אַף הַמַּזִּיקִין, וּקְבוּרָתוֹ שֶׁל מֹשֶׁה, וְאֵילוֹ שֶׁל אַבְרָהָם אָבִינוּ. וְיֵשׁ אוֹמְרִים, אַף צְבָת בִּצְבָת עֲשׂוּיָה:

ז שִׁבְעָה דְבָרִים בַּגֹּלֶם וְשִׁבְעָה בֶחָכָם. חָכָם אֵינוֹ מְדַבֵּר בִּפְנֵי מִי שֶׁהוּא גָדוֹל מִמֶּנּוּ בְּחָכְמָה וּבְמִנְיָן, וְאֵינוֹ נִכְנָס לְתוֹךְ דִּבְרֵי חֲבֵרוֹ, וְאֵינוֹ נִבְהָל לְהָשִׁיב, שׁוֹאֵל כָּעִנְיָן וּמֵשִׁיב כַּהֲלָכָה, וְאוֹמֵר עַל רִאשׁוֹן רִאשׁוֹן וְעַל אַחֲרוֹן אַחֲרוֹן, וְעַל מַה שֶּׁלֹּא שָׁמַע, אוֹמֵר לֹא שָׁמָעְתִּי, וּמוֹדֶה עַל הָאֱמֶת. וְחִלּוּפֵיהֶן בַּגֹּלֶם:

ח שִׁבְעָה מִינֵי פֻרְעָנִיּוֹת בָּאִין לָעוֹלָם עַל שִׁבְעָה גוּפֵי עֲבֵרָה. מִקְצָתָן מְעַשְּׂרִין וּמִקְצָתָן אֵינָן מְעַשְּׂרִין, רָעָב שֶׁל בַּצֹּרֶת בָּאָה, מִקְצָתָן רְעֵבִים וּמִקְצָתָן שְׂבֵעִים. גָּמְרוּ שֶׁלֹּא לְעַשֵּׂר, רָעָב שֶׁל מְהוּמָה וְשֶׁל בַּצֹּרֶת בָּאָה. וְשֶׁלֹּא לִטּוֹל אֶת הַחַלָּה, רָעָב שֶׁל כְּלָיָה בָּאָה. דֶּבֶר בָּא לָעוֹלָם עַל מִיתוֹת הָאֲמוּרוֹת בַּתּוֹרָה שֶׁלֹּא נִמְסְרוּ לְבֵית דִּין, וְעַל פֵּרוֹת

any [human] court and for [transgressions involving] the seventh-year produce. The sword comes into the world because of justice delayed and justice denied and because of those who misinterpret the Torah.

5:9 Wild animals come to the world [to attack people] because of false swearing and the profaning of God's name. Exile comes to the world because of idolatry, sexual impropriety, bloodshed, and the [neglect of the sabbatical] release of the land. Pestilence increases during four periods: in the fourth year, in the seventh year, in the year following that year, and each year at the end of the Festival [of Sukkot]. The fourth year [increase] is because of [the failure to give] the tithe for the poor due in the sixth year. [The increase] in the year following is because of [transgressing the laws of] the seventh-year produce. [The increase] following each Festival [of Sukkot] is because of the theft of what is due to the poor.

5:10 There are four kinds of human beings. One says, "What is mine is mine and what is yours is yours." That is the usual kind, although some say that is the Sodom kind. [The one who says,] "What is mine is yours and what is yours is mine" is an ignoramus. [The one who says,] "What is mine is yours and what is yours is yours" is a saint. [And the one who says,] "What is mine is mine and what is yours is mine" is a sinner.

5:11 There are four kinds of dispositions: [One is] easy to anger and easy to calm. That one's gain is nullified by the loss. [One is] hard to anger and hard to calm. That one's loss is nullified by the gain. [One is] hard to anger and easy to calm. That one is a saint. [The last is] easy to anger and hard to calm. That one is a sinner.

5:12 There are four kinds of students. One is quick to learn and quick to forget. What that one gains, that one loses. One is slow to learn but slow to forget. What that one loses, that one gains. One learns quickly and is slow to forget. [Such a person will be] a scholar. Regarding the one who is slow to learn and quick to forget, that one will have a bad portion.

5:13 There are four kinds of people who would give to charity. One wishes to give but [believes] that others should not. That one's eye is evil to those others. One [wishes that] others give and that he should not. His eye is evil toward himself. One [wishes that] he should give and so should others. That one is a saint. [The] one [who believes that he] should not give nor should others is a sinner.

5:14 There are four kinds of persons who would go to the house of study. One goes but does not practice. [This one] has the reward for going. One practices but does not go. [This one] gets the reward for practice. The one who goes and practices is a saint. The one who neither goes nor practices is a sinner.

שְׁבִיעִית. חֶרֶב בָּאָה לָעוֹלָם עַל עִנּוּי הַדִּין,
וְעַל עִוּוּת הַדִּין, וְעַל הַמּוֹרִים בַּתּוֹרָה שֶׁלֹּא כַהֲלָכָה:

ט חַיָּה רָעָה בָּאָה לָעוֹלָם עַל שְׁבוּעַת שָׁוְא,
וְעַל חִלּוּל הַשֵּׁם. גָּלוּת בָּאָה לָעוֹלָם עַל עוֹבְדֵי עֲבוֹדָה זָרָה,
וְעַל גִּלּוּי עֲרָיוֹת, וְעַל שְׁפִיכוּת דָּמִים,
וְעַל הַשְׁמָטַת הָאָרֶץ. בְּאַרְבָּעָה פְרָקִים הַדֶּבֶר מִתְרַבֶּה.
בָּרְבִיעִית, וּבַשְּׁבִיעִית, וּבְמוֹצָאֵי שְׁבִיעִית,
וּבְמוֹצָאֵי הֶחָג שֶׁבְּכָל שָׁנָה וְשָׁנָה. בָּרְבִיעִית, מִפְּנֵי מַעְשַׂר
עָנִי שֶׁבַּשְּׁלִישִׁית. בַּשְּׁבִיעִית, מִפְּנֵי מַעְשַׂר
עָנִי שֶׁבַּשִּׁשִּׁית. וּבְמוֹצָאֵי שְׁבִיעִית, מִפְּנֵי פֵרוֹת שְׁבִיעִית.
וּבְמוֹצָאֵי הֶחָג שֶׁבְּכָל שָׁנָה וְשָׁנָה, מִפְּנֵי גֶזֶל מַתְּנוֹת עֲנִיִּים:

י אַרְבַּע מִדּוֹת בָּאָדָם. הָאוֹמֵר שֶׁלִּי שֶׁלִּי וְשֶׁלְּךָ
שֶׁלָּךְ, זוֹ מִדָּה בֵּינוֹנִית. וְיֵשׁ אוֹמְרִים, זוֹ מִדַּת
סְדוֹם. שֶׁלִּי שֶׁלָּךְ וְשֶׁלְּךָ שֶׁלִּי, עַם הָאָרֶץ.
שֶׁלִּי שֶׁלָּךְ וְשֶׁלְּךָ שֶׁלָּךְ, חָסִיד. שֶׁלִּי שֶׁלִּי
וְשֶׁלְּךָ שֶׁלִּי, רָשָׁע:

יא אַרְבַּע מִדּוֹת בַּדֵּעוֹת. נוֹחַ לִכְעוֹס וְנוֹחַ
לִרְצוֹת, יָצָא שְׂכָרוֹ בְהֶפְסֵדוֹ, קָשֶׁה לִכְעוֹס
וְקָשֶׁה לִרְצוֹת, יָצָא הֶפְסֵדוֹ בִשְׂכָרוֹ קָשֶׁה
לִכְעוֹס וְנוֹחַ לִרְצוֹת חָסִיד. נוֹחַ לִכְעוֹס וְקָשֶׁה
לִרְצוֹת רָשָׁע:

יב אַרְבַּע מִדּוֹת בַּתַּלְמִידִים. מַהֵר לִשְׁמוֹעַ
וּמַהֵר לְאַבֵּד, יָצָא שְׂכָרוֹ בְהֶפְסֵדוֹ. קָשֶׁה
לִשְׁמוֹעַ וְקָשֶׁה לְאַבֵּד, יָצָא הֶפְסֵדוֹ בִשְׂכָרוֹ.
מַהֵר לִשְׁמוֹעַ וְקָשֶׁה לְאַבֵּד, חָכָם. קָשֶׁה
לִשְׁמוֹעַ וּמַהֵר לְאַבֵּד, זֶה חֵלֶק רָע:

יג אַרְבַּע מִדּוֹת בְּנוֹתְנֵי צְדָקָה. הָרוֹצֶה שֶׁיִּתֵּן
וְלֹא יִתְּנוּ אֲחֵרִים, עֵינוֹ רָעָה בְּשֶׁל אֲחֵרִים.
יִתְּנוּ אֲחֵרִים וְהוּא לֹא יִתֵּן, עֵינוֹ רָעָה בְּשֶׁלּוֹ.
יִתֵּן וְיִתְּנוּ אֲחֵרִים, חָסִיד.
לֹא יִתֵּן וְלֹא יִתְּנוּ אֲחֵרִים, רָשָׁע:

יד אַרְבַּע מִדּוֹת בְּהוֹלְכֵי לְבֵית הַמִּדְרָשׁ. הוֹלֵךְ
וְאֵינוֹ עוֹשֶׂה, שְׂכַר הֲלִיכָה בְיָדוֹ. עוֹשֶׂה וְאֵינוֹ
הוֹלֵךְ, שְׂכַר מַעֲשֶׂה בְיָדוֹ. הוֹלֵךְ וְעוֹשֶׂה,
חָסִיד. לֹא הוֹלֵךְ וְלֹא עוֹשֶׂה, רָשָׁע:

5:15 There are four kinds [of disciples] who sit before the sages: the sponge, the funnel, the strainer, and the sieve. The sponge soaks up everything. The funnel takes in at one end and pours out the other. The strainer lets out the wine and keeps the dregs. The sieve lets out the flour [dust] and keeps the fine flour.

5:16 When love depends on something [beyond itself], when that something [beyond itself] disappears, that love disappears. However, when love does not depend on something [beyond itself], that love will never disappear. Which love depended on something [beyond itself]? The love between Amnon and Tamar. Which love did not depend on something [beyond itself]? The love of David and Jonathan.

5:17 Any controversy that is for the sake of Heaven shall in the end be resolved. A controversy that is not for the sake of Heaven shall not be resolved. Which controversy was for the sake of Heaven? [The controversy] between Hillel and Shammai. Which controversy was not for the sake of Heaven? [The controversy] of Korach and his band.

5:18 No sin will occur through any individual who would bring people to righteousness. No repentance will be possible to any person who would cause the multitude to sin. Moses was meritorious and made the multitude meritorious. Their merit was attributed to him, as it says, "He executed the righteousness of *Adonai* and divine ordinances of Israel." [Deut. 33:21] Yaravam, the son of Nevat, sinned and caused the multitude to sin. The sin of the multitude is attributed to him, as it says, "For the sins of Yaravam that he sinned and caused Israel to sin." [1 Kings 15:30]

5:19 Whoever possesses the following three qualities is a disciple of Abraham our patriarch. Whoever possesses the following three [opposite] qualities is a disciple of Balaam the wicked. A good eye, a humble spirit, a restricted desire, [these belong] to the disciples of Abraham. An evil eye, a proud spirit, and an unrestricted desire [belong to] the disciples of Balaam the wicked. What is the difference between the disciples of Abraham and the disciples of Balaam? The disciples of Abraham enjoy this world and will inherit the world to come, as it says, "That I may cause those who love Me to inherit substance and that I may fill their treasuries." [Prov. 8:21] The disciples of Balaam the wicked will inherit *Gehinnom* and will go down into the pit of destruction, as it says, "But You, O God, will bring them down into the pit of destruction; bloodthirsty and deceitful people will not live out half their days." [Ps. 55:24]

5:20 Yehudah ben Tema used to say, "Be as strong as a leopard, as quick as an eagle, as fast as a deer, and as brave as a lion to do the will of your Parent in heaven." He used to say, "The shameless [will go] to *Gehinnom* and the shamefaced [will go] to *Gan Eden. Adonai* our God, may it be Your will that Your city will be speedily built in our days. Grant our portion in Your Torah."

טו אַרְבַּע מִדּוֹת בְּיוֹשְׁבִים לִפְנֵי חֲכָמִים. סְפוֹג, וּמַשְׁפֵּךְ, מְשַׁמֶּרֶת, וְנָפָה. סְפוֹג, שֶׁהוּא סוֹפֵג אֶת הַכֹּל. מַשְׁפֵּךְ, שֶׁמַּכְנִיס בְּזוֹ וּמוֹצִיא בְזוֹ. מְשַׁמֶּרֶת, שֶׁמּוֹצִיאָה אֶת הַיַּיִן וְקוֹלֶטֶת אֶת הַשְּׁמָרִים. וְנָפָה, שֶׁמּוֹצִיאָה אֶת הַקֶּמַח וְקוֹלֶטֶת אֶת הַסֹּלֶת:

טז כָּל אַהֲבָה שֶׁהִיא תְלוּיָה בְדָבָר, בָּטֵל דָּבָר, בְּטֵלָה אַהֲבָה. וְשֶׁאֵינָה תְלוּיָה בְדָבָר, אֵינָהּ בְּטֵלָה לְעוֹלָם. אֵיזוֹ הִיא אַהֲבָה הַתְּלוּיָה בְדָבָר, זוֹ אַהֲבַת אַמְנוֹן וְתָמָר. וְשֶׁאֵינָהּ תְלוּיָה בְדָבָר, זוֹ אַהֲבַת דָּוִד וִיהוֹנָתָן:

יז כָּל מַחֲלוֹקֶת שֶׁהִיא לְשֵׁם שָׁמַיִם, סוֹפָהּ לְהִתְקַיֵּם. וְשֶׁאֵינָהּ לְשֵׁם שָׁמַיִם, אֵין סוֹפָהּ לְהִתְקַיֵּם. אֵיזוֹ הִיא מַחֲלוֹקֶת שֶׁהִיא לְשֵׁם שָׁמַיִם, זוֹ מַחֲלוֹקֶת הִלֵּל וְשַׁמַּאי. וְשֶׁאֵינָהּ לְשֵׁם שָׁמַיִם, זוֹ מַחֲלוֹקֶת קֹרַח וְכָל עֲדָתוֹ:

יח כָּל הַמְזַכֶּה אֶת הָרַבִּים, אֵין חֵטְא בָּא עַל יָדוֹ. וְכָל הַמַּחֲטִיא אֶת הָרַבִּים, אֵין מַסְפִּיקִין בְּיָדוֹ לַעֲשׂוֹת תְּשׁוּבָה. מֹשֶׁה זָכָה וְזִכָּה אֶת הָרַבִּים, זְכוּת הָרַבִּים תָּלוּי בּוֹ, שֶׁנֶּאֱמַר (דברים לג), צִדְקַת ה' עָשָׂה וּמִשְׁפָּטָיו עִם יִשְׂרָאֵל. יָרָבְעָם חָטָא וְהֶחֱטִיא אֶת הָרַבִּים, חֵטְא הָרַבִּים תָּלוּי בּוֹ, שֶׁנֶּאֱמַר (מלכים א טו), עַל חַטֹּאות יָרָבְעָם אֲשֶׁר חָטָא וַאֲשֶׁר הֶחֱטִיא אֶת יִשְׂרָאֵל:

יט כָּל מִי שֶׁיֵּשׁ בְּיָדוֹ שְׁלֹשָׁה דְבָרִים הַלָּלוּ, מִתַּלְמִידָיו שֶׁל אַבְרָהָם אָבִינוּ. וּשְׁלֹשָׁה דְבָרִים אֲחֵרִים, מִתַּלְמִידָיו שֶׁל בִּלְעָם הָרָשָׁע. עַיִן טוֹבָה, וְרוּחַ נְמוּכָה, וְנֶפֶשׁ שְׁפָלָה, מִתַּלְמִידָיו שֶׁל אַבְרָהָם אָבִינוּ. עַיִן רָעָה, וְרוּחַ גְּבוֹהָה, וְנֶפֶשׁ רְחָבָה, מִתַּלְמִידָיו שֶׁל בִּלְעָם הָרָשָׁע. מַה בֵּין תַּלְמִידָיו שֶׁל אַבְרָהָם אָבִינוּ לְתַלְמִידָיו שֶׁל בִּלְעָם הָרָשָׁע. תַּלְמִידָיו שֶׁל אַבְרָהָם אָבִינוּ, אוֹכְלִין בָּעוֹלָם הַזֶּה וְנוֹחֲלִין בָּעוֹלָם הַבָּא, שֶׁנֶּאֱמַר (משלי ח), לְהַנְחִיל אֹהֲבַי יֵשׁ, וְאֹצְרֹתֵיהֶם אֲמַלֵּא. אֲבָל תַּלְמִידָיו שֶׁל בִּלְעָם הָרָשָׁע יוֹרְשִׁין גֵּיהִנָּם וְיוֹרְדִין לִבְאֵר שַׁחַת, שֶׁנֶּאֱמַר (תהלים נה), וְאַתָּה אֱלֹהִים תּוֹרִדֵם לִבְאֵר שַׁחַת, אַנְשֵׁי דָמִים וּמִרְמָה לֹא יֶחֱצוּ יְמֵיהֶם, וַאֲנִי אֶבְטַח בָּךְ:

כ יְהוּדָה בֶן תֵּימָא אוֹמֵר, הֱוֵי עַז כַּנָּמֵר, וְקַל כַּנֶּשֶׁר, וְרָץ כַּצְּבִי, וְגִבּוֹר כָּאֲרִי לַעֲשׂוֹת רְצוֹן אָבִיךְ שֶׁבַּשָּׁמָיִם. הוּא הָיָה אוֹמֵר, עַז פָּנִים לְגֵיהִנָּם, וּבֹשֶׁת פָּנִים לְגַן עֵדֶן. יְהִי רָצוֹן מִלְּפָנֶיךָ יְיָ אֱלֹהֵינוּ שֶׁתִּבָּנֶה עִירְךָ בִּמְהֵרָה בְיָמֵינוּ וְתֵן חֶלְקֵנוּ בְתוֹרָתֶךָ:

5:21 He used to say, "At five [one begins the study of] the Bible. At ten the *Mishnah*. At thirteen [one takes on] the [responsibility for] the *mitzvot*. At fifteen [one begins the study of] the Talmud. At eighteen [one is ready for] marriage. At twenty to pursue [a livelihood]. At thirty [one attains full] strength. At forty [one gains] understanding. At fifty [one gives] counsel. At sixty [one reaches] old age. At seventy [one reaches] the fullness of age. At eighty [one reaches] strong old age. At ninety [one is] bent. And, at one hundred, it is as if one had already died and passed from the world.

5:22 Ben Bag Bag used to say, "Turn it, and turn it, for everything is in it. Reflect on it and grow old and gray with it. Don't turn from it, for nothing is better than it."

5:23 Ben Hei Hei said, "According to the difficulty is the reward."

Chapter 6

The sages taught [the following] in the style of the *Mishnah*. Blessed be the One who chose them and their teaching.

6:1 Rabbi Meir said, "Whoever studies the Torah for its own sake merits many things. Indeed the entire world is rendered worthy for this one's sake. This one is called friend, beloved, one who loves God, one who loves humankind, one who pleases God, and one who pleases humankind. [The Torah] clothes this person in humility and reverence and prepares the person to be righteous and pious, upright, and trustworthy. It keeps the individual far from sin and brings this person near to merit. From this person others gain counsel and wisdom, understanding and strength, as it says, 'Counsel and wisdom are mine [the Torah's]. I am understanding. Strength is mine.' [Prov. 8:14] It gives the individual sovereignty and dominion and the ability to judge. To this person the secrets of the Torah are revealed so that this person becomes like an ever-flowing spring, like a river that never dries up. This person becomes modest and patient and forgiving of insults. [The Torah] makes this person great and raises this person above all things."

6:2 Rabbi Yehoshua ben Levi would say, "Every day a heavenly voice proceeds from Mount Chorev and proclaims, 'Woe to all humans because of their contempt for the Torah!' One who does not occupy oneself with the Torah is called a reprobate, as it says, 'As a gold ring in a swine's snout, so is a beautiful woman without sense.' [Prov. 11:22] Another verse says, 'And the tablets were the work of God and the writing was the writing of God, which was engraved on the tablets.' [Exod. 32:16] Don't read 'engraved' [*charut*] but rather [read] 'freedom' [*cherut*], for only the individual who is engaged in the study of Torah is [truly] free. That person who is engaged in the regular study of Torah is exalted as it says, 'And from Mattanah to Nachaliel and from Nachaliel to Bamot.'" [Num. 21:19]

כא הוּא הָיָה אוֹמֵר, בֶּן חָמֵשׁ שָׁנִים לַמִּקְרָא, בֶּן עֶשֶׂר לַמִּשְׁנָה, בֶּן שְׁלֹשׁ עֶשְׂרֵה לַמִּצְוֹת, בֶּן חֲמֵשׁ עֶשְׂרֵה לַתַּלְמוּד, בֶּן שְׁמֹנָה עֶשְׂרֵה לַחֻפָּה, בֶּן עֶשְׂרִים לִרְדּוֹף, בֶּן שְׁלֹשִׁים לַכֹּחַ, בֶּן אַרְבָּעִים לַבִּינָה, בֶּן חֲמִשִּׁים לָעֵצָה, בֶּן שִׁשִּׁים לַזִּקְנָה, בֶּן שִׁבְעִים לַשֵּׂיבָה, בֶּן שְׁמֹנִים לַגְּבוּרָה, בֶּן תִּשְׁעִים לָשׁוּחַ, בֶּן מֵאָה כְּאִלּוּ מֵת וְעָבַר וּבָטֵל מִן הָעוֹלָם:

כב בֶּן בַּג בַּג אוֹמֵר, הֲפָךְ בָּהּ וַהֲפָךְ בָּהּ, דְּכֹלָּא בָהּ. וּבָהּ תֶּחֱזֵי, וְסִיב וּבְלֵה בַהּ, וּמִנַּהּ לָא תְזוּעַ, שֶׁאֵין לְךָ מִדָּה טוֹבָה הֵימֶנָּה:

כג בֶּן הֵא הֵא אוֹמֵר, לְפוּם צַעֲרָא אַגְרָא:

פרק ו

שָׁנוּ חֲכָמִים בִּלְשׁוֹן הַמִּשְׁנָה, בָּרוּךְ שֶׁבָּחַר בָּהֶם וּבְמִשְׁנָתָם:

א רַבִּי מֵאִיר אוֹמֵר כָּל הָעוֹסֵק בַּתּוֹרָה לִשְׁמָהּ, זוֹכֶה לִדְבָרִים הַרְבֵּה. וְלֹא עוֹד אֶלָּא שֶׁכָּל הָעוֹלָם כֻּלּוֹ כְּדַאי הוּא לוֹ. נִקְרָא רֵעַ, אָהוּב, אוֹהֵב אֶת הַמָּקוֹם, אוֹהֵב אֶת הַבְּרִיּוֹת, מְשַׂמֵּחַ אֶת הַמָּקוֹם, מְשַׂמֵּחַ אֶת הַבְּרִיּוֹת, וּמַלְבַּשְׁתּוֹ עֲנָוָה וְיִרְאָה, וּמַכְשַׁרְתּוֹ לִהְיוֹת צַדִּיק חָסִיד יָשָׁר וְנֶאֱמָן, וּמְרַחַקְתּוֹ מִן הַחֵטְא, וּמְקָרַבְתּוֹ לִידֵי זְכוּת, וְנֶהֱנִין מִמֶּנּוּ עֵצָה וְתוּשִׁיָּה בִּינָה וּגְבוּרָה. שֶׁנֶּאֱמַר (משלי ח) לִי עֵצָה וְתוּשִׁיָּה אֲנִי בִינָה לִי גְבוּרָה, וְנוֹתֶנֶת לוֹ מַלְכוּת וּמֶמְשָׁלָה וְחִקּוּר דִּין, וּמְגַלִּין לוֹ רָזֵי תוֹרָה, וְנַעֲשֶׂה כְּמַעְיָן הַמִּתְגַּבֵּר וּכְנָהָר שֶׁאֵינוֹ פוֹסֵק, וֶהֱוֵי צָנוּעַ וְאֶרֶךְ רוּחַ, וּמוֹחֵל עַל עֶלְבּוֹנוֹ, וּמְגַדַּלְתּוֹ וּמְרוֹמַמְתּוֹ עַל כָּל הַמַּעֲשִׂים:

ב אָמַר רַבִּי יְהוֹשֻׁעַ בֶּן לֵוִי, בְּכָל יוֹם וָיוֹם בַּת קוֹל יוֹצֵאת מֵהַר חוֹרֵב וּמַכְרֶזֶת וְאוֹמֶרֶת אוֹי לָהֶם לַבְּרִיּוֹת מֵעֶלְבּוֹנָהּ שֶׁל תּוֹרָה. שֶׁכָּל מִי שֶׁאֵינוֹ עוֹסֵק בַּתּוֹרָה נִקְרָא נָזוּף, שֶׁנֶּאֱמַר (שם יא) נֶזֶם זָהָב בְּאַף חֲזִיר אִשָּׁה יָפָה וְסָרַת טָעַם. וְאוֹמֵר (שמות לב), וְהַלֻּחֹת מַעֲשֵׂה אֱלֹהִים הֵמָּה וְהַמִּכְתָּב מִכְתַּב אֱלֹהִים הוּא חָרוּת עַל הַלֻּחֹת, אַל תִּקְרָא חָרוּת אֶלָּא חֵרוּת, שֶׁאֵין לְךָ בֶּן חוֹרִין אֶלָּא מִי שֶׁעוֹסֵק בְּתַלְמוּד תּוֹרָה. וְכָל מִי שֶׁעוֹסֵק בְּתַלְמוּד תּוֹרָה הֲרֵי זֶה מִתְעַלֶּה, שֶׁנֶּאֱמַר (במדבר כא) וּמִמַּתָּנָה נַחֲלִיאֵל וּמִנַּחֲלִיאֵל בָּמוֹת:

6:3 Whoever learns from another, one chapter or one law or one verse or one word or even one letter, is bound to accord the teacher honor. We learn this from King David who learned only two things from Achitophel but called him teacher, companion, and friend, as it says, "You are my equal, my companion, and my familiar friend." [Ps. 55:14] There is certainly an inference to be drawn. If David, king of Israel, learned only two things from Achitophel and regarded him as his teacher, companion, and friend, how much the more should one who learns a chapter, a law, a verse, a word, or even a letter from another accord that other [person such] honor. Honor can only mean Torah as it says, "The wise shall inherit honor" [Prov. 3:35] [and] "The perfect shall inherit good." [Prov. 28:10] *Good* means *Torah*, as it says, "I give you good doctrine, do not forsake My Torah." [Prov. 4:2]

6:4 This is the way of the [study] of the Torah: you will eat bread with salt. You will drink water by measure, you will endure a life of privation. [All] while you labor in the Torah. If you do this, "Happy shall you be and good will be yours." [Ps. 128:2] Happy shall you be in this world and good will be yours in the world to come. Don't seek greatness for yourself and don't covet glory. More than you've learned, do! Don't hanker after the tables of kings for your table is greater than theirs. Your crown is grander than theirs. [Only] your Employer can be depended on to pay you the reward of your labor.

6:5 [The requirements for] the Torah are greater than those for the priesthood or for royalty. Royalty is acquired by thirty qualities and the priesthood by twenty-four. The Torah [on the other hand] is acquired by forty-eight: study; careful listening; vocal repetition; insight; mental acuity; awe; reverence; humility; joy; service to the sages; association with fellow students; arguing with the disciples; self-control; [the knowledge of] the Bible and the *Mishnah*; moderation in business, in sleep, in speech, in pleasure, in laughter, in worldly affairs; by being patient; by having a good heart; by having trust in the sages; and by the acceptance of suffering.

6:6 [Knowledge of Torah is acquired by] the one who knows one's place, who rejoices in one's portion, who sets a limit to one's words, who claims no credit for oneself, who is beloved, who loves God, who loves people, who loves justice, who loves reproof, who loves equity, who distances oneself from glory, who does not arrogantly show off learning, who does not enjoy judging, who bears the yoke with one's colleague, who judges the colleague favorably, [even while] directing that person to truth and peace, the one whose study has calmed the mind, who asks and answers, who listens and adds, who studies in order to teach and who studies in order to practice, who makes one's teacher wiser, who reports exactly what has been learned, and who quotes a teaching in the name of the one who said it. Behold you have learned that who reports something in the name of the one who said it brings redemption into the

ג הַלוֹמֵד מֵחֲבֵרוֹ פֶּרֶק אֶחָד אוֹ הֲלָכָה אַחַת אוֹ פָּסוּק אֶחָד אוֹ דִבּוּר אֶחָד אוֹ אֲפִלּוּ אוֹת אֶחָת, צָרִיךְ לִנְהָג בּוֹ כָּבוֹד, שֶׁכֵּן מָצִינוּ בְּדָוִד מֶלֶךְ יִשְׂרָאֵל, שֶׁלֹּא לָמַד מֵאֲחִיתֹפֶל אֶלָּא שְׁנֵי דְבָרִים בִּלְבַד, קְרָאוֹ רַבּוֹ אַלּוּפוֹ וּמְיֻדָּעוֹ, שֶׁנֶּאֱמַר (תהלים נה), וְאַתָּה אֱנוֹשׁ כְּעֶרְכִּי אַלּוּפִי וּמְיֻדָּעִי. וַהֲלֹא דְבָרִים קַל וָחֹמֶר, וּמַה דָּוִד מֶלֶךְ יִשְׂרָאֵל שֶׁלֹּא לָמַד מֵאֲחִיתֹפֶל אֶלָּא שְׁנֵי דְבָרִים בִּלְבַד קְרָאוֹ רַבּוֹ אַלּוּפוֹ וּמְיֻדָּעוֹ, הַלוֹמֵד מֵחֲבֵרוֹ פֶּרֶק אֶחָד אוֹ הֲלָכָה אַחַת אוֹ פָּסוּק אֶחָד אוֹ דִבּוּר אֶחָד אוֹ אֲפִלּוּ אוֹת אֶחַת עַל אַחַת כַּמָּה וְכַמָּה שֶׁצָּרִיךְ לִנְהָג בּוֹ כָּבוֹד. וְאֵין כָּבוֹד אֶלָּא תוֹרָה, שֶׁנֶּאֱמַר (משלי ג), כָּבוֹד חֲכָמִים יִנְחָלוּ, (שם כח) וּתְמִימִים יִנְחֲלוּ טוֹב, וְאֵין טוֹב אֶלָּא תוֹרָה שֶׁנֶּאֱמַר כִּי לֶקַח טוֹב נָתַתִּי לָכֶם תּוֹרָתִי אַל תַּעֲזֹבוּ:

ד כַּךְ הִיא דַּרְכָּהּ שֶׁל תּוֹרָה, פַּת בַּמֶּלַח תֹּאכֵל וּמַיִם בַּמְּשׂוּרָה תִשְׁתֶּה וְעַל הָאָרֶץ תִּישָׁן וְחַיֵּי צַעַר תִּחְיֶה וּבַתּוֹרָה אַתָּה עָמֵל, אִם אַתָּה עֹשֶׂה כֵן, (תהלים קכח) אַשְׁרֶיךָ וְטוֹב לָךְ. אַשְׁרֶיךָ בָּעוֹלָם הַזֶּה וְטוֹב לָךְ לָעוֹלָם הַבָּא: אַל תְּבַקֵּשׁ גְּדֻלָּה לְעַצְמְךָ, וְאַל תַּחְמֹד כָּבוֹד, יוֹתֵר מִלִּמּוּדְךָ עֲשֵׂה, וְאַל תִּתְאַוֶּה לְשֻׁלְחָנָם שֶׁל שָׂרִים, שֶׁשֻּׁלְחָנְךָ גָּדוֹל מִשֻּׁלְחָנָם וְכִתְרְךָ גָּדוֹל מִכִּתְרָם, וְנֶאֱמָן הוּא בַּעַל מְלַאכְתְּךָ שֶׁיְּשַׁלֶּם לָךְ שְׂכַר פְּעֻלָּתֶךָ:

ה גְּדוֹלָה תוֹרָה יוֹתֵר מִן הַכְּהֻנָּה וּמִן הַמַּלְכוּת, שֶׁהַמַּלְכוּת נִקְנֵית בִּשְׁלֹשִׁים מַעֲלוֹת, וְהַכְּהֻנָּה בְּעֶשְׂרִים וְאַרְבַּע, וְהַתּוֹרָה נִקְנֵית בְּאַרְבָּעִים וּשְׁמוֹנָה דְבָרִים. וְאֵלּוּ הֵן, בְּתַלְמוּד, בִּשְׁמִיעַת הָאֹזֶן, בַּעֲרִיכַת שְׂפָתַיִם, בְּבִינַת הַלֵּב, בְּאֵימָה, בְּיִרְאָה, בַּעֲנָוָה, בְּשִׂמְחָה, בְּטָהֳרָה, בְּשִׁמּוּשׁ חֲכָמִים, בְּדִקְדּוּק חֲבֵרִים, בְּפִלְפּוּל הַתַּלְמִידִים, בְּיִשּׁוּב, בְּמִקְרָא, בְּמִשְׁנָה, בְּמִעוּט סְחוֹרָה, בְּמִעוּט דֶּרֶךְ אֶרֶץ, בְּמִעוּט תַּעֲנוּג, בְּמִעוּט שֵׁנָה, בְּמִעוּט שִׂיחָה, בְּמִעוּט שְׂחוֹק, בְּאֶרֶךְ אַפַּיִם, בְּלֵב טוֹב, בֶּאֱמוּנַת חֲכָמִים, בְּקַבָּלַת הַיִּסּוּרִין.

ו הַמַּכִּיר אֶת מְקוֹמוֹ, וְהַשָּׂמֵחַ בְּחֶלְקוֹ, וְהָעוֹשֶׂה סְיָג לִדְבָרָיו, וְאֵינוֹ מַחֲזִיק טוֹבָה לְעַצְמוֹ, אָהוּב, אוֹהֵב אֶת הַמָּקוֹם, אוֹהֵב אֶת הַבְּרִיּוֹת, אוֹהֵב אֶת הַצְּדָקוֹת, אוֹהֵב אֶת הַמֵּישָׁרִים, אוֹהֵב אֶת הַתּוֹכָחוֹת, וּמִתְרַחֵק מִן הַכָּבוֹד, וְלֹא מֵגִיס לִבּוֹ בְּתַלְמוּדוֹ, וְאֵינוֹ שָׂמֵחַ בְּהוֹרָאָה, נוֹשֵׂא בְעֹל עִם חֲבֵרוֹ, וּמַכְרִיעוֹ לְכַף זְכוּת, וּמַעֲמִידוֹ עַל הָאֱמֶת, וּמַעֲמִידוֹ עַל הַשָּׁלוֹם, וּמִתְיַשֵּׁב לִבּוֹ בְּתַלְמוּדוֹ, שׁוֹאֵל וּמֵשִׁיב שׁוֹמֵעַ וּמוֹסִיף, הַלּוֹמֵד עַל מְנָת לְלַמֵּד וְהַלּוֹמֵד עַל מְנָת לַעֲשׂוֹת, הַמַּחְכִּים אֶת רַבּוֹ, וְהַמְכַוֵּן אֶת שְׁמוּעָתוֹ, וְהָאוֹמֵר דָּבָר בְּשֵׁם אוֹמְרוֹ, הָא לָמַדְתָּ כָּל הָאוֹמֵר דָּבָר בְּשֵׁם אוֹמְרוֹ מֵבִיא גְאֻלָּה לָעוֹלָם,

world as it says, "And Esther said in the name of Mordecai." [Esther 2:22]

6:7 Great is the Torah because it gives life to those who perform it in this world and in the next as it says, "For they are life to them that find them, and healing to all their flesh." [Prov. 4:22] And it says, "It shall be health to your navel and marrow to your bones." [Prov. 3:8] And it says, "It is a tree of life to all who hold fast to it and all its supporters are happy." [Prov. 3:18] And it also says, "They are a chaplet of grace for your head and chains around your neck." [Prov. 1:9] And it says, "It shall give you a chaplet of grace; a crown of glory shall it give you." [Prov. 4:9] And it says, "By me your days will be multiplied and the years of your life increased." [Prov. 9:11] And it says, "Length of days is in her right hand; riches and honor are in her left hand." [Prov. 3:16] And it says, "For length of days and years of life and peace shall be added to you." [Prov. 3:2]

6:8 Rabbi Shimon ben Menasya said in the name of Rabbi Shimon bar Yochai, "Beauty, strength, wealth, honor, wisdom, old age, gray hair [advanced age], and children befit the righteous and befit the world, as it says, 'Gray hair is a crown of glory; in the way of righteousness, it may be found.'" [Prov. 16:31] Another verse says, "Wealth is the crown of the wise." [Prov. 14:24] Still another verse says, "Grandchildren are the crown of the old while their parents are the glory of children." [Prov. 17:6] Yet another verse says, "Strength is the glory of the young while gray hair is the beauty of the old." [Prov. 20:29] A final verse says, "The moon will be confounded and the sun ashamed, for *Adonai Tzevaot* will reign on Mount Zion and in Jerusalem. And before God's elders will be glory." [Isa. 24:23] Rabbi Shimon be Menasya said, "These seven qualities that the sages attributed to the righteous were all realized in Rabbi [Yehudah Ha-Nasi] and his sons."

6:9 Rabbi Yose ben Kisma said, "Once I was traveling and a man met me and greeted me. When I returned his greeting, he said to me, 'Rabbi, where do you come from?' I replied, 'From a great city of sages and scholars.' He then said, 'Rabbi, would you be willing to live with us in our place? [If you would] I would give you a million golden dinars along with precious stones and pearls!' I said to him, 'Were you to give me all the silver and gold and precious stones and pearls in the world, I would live only in a place of Torah!' Thus it is written in the Book or Psalms by the hand of David, king of Israel, 'The Torah of your mouth is better to me than thousands of gold and silver.' [Ps. 119:72] Not only that, but, at the moment of a person's departure [from this world], neither silver nor gold nor precious stones nor pearls accompany the individual, only Torah and good deeds, as it says, 'When you walk, it will guide you; when you lie down, it will watch over you; and when you awake, it will speak to you.' [Prov. 6:22] 'When you walk, it will guide you'–in this world. 'When you lie down, it will watch over you'–in the grave. 'And when you awake, it will speak to you'–in the world to come. Moreover, it

שֶׁנֶּאֱמַר (אסתר ב), וַתֹּאמֶר אֶסְתֵּר לַמֶּלֶךְ בְּשֵׁם מָרְדְּכָי:

ז גְּדוֹלָה תוֹרָה שֶׁהִיא נוֹתֶנֶת חַיִּים לְעוֹשֶׂיהָ בָּעוֹלָם הַזֶּה וּבָעוֹלָם הַבָּא, שֶׁנֶּאֱמַר (משלי ד), כִּי חַיִּים הֵם לְמוֹצְאֵיהֶם וּלְכָל בְּשָׂרוֹ מַרְפֵּא, וְאוֹמֵר (שם ג), רִפְאוּת תְּהִי לְשָׁרֶּךָ וְשִׁקּוּי לְעַצְמוֹתֶיךָ. וְאוֹמֵר (שם), עֵץ חַיִּים הִיא לַמַּחֲזִיקִים בָּהּ וְתוֹמְכֶיהָ מְאֻשָּׁר. וְאוֹמֵר (שם א), כִּי לִוְיַת חֵן הֵם לְרֹאשֶׁךָ וַעֲנָקִים לְגַרְגְּרֹתֶיךָ. וְאוֹמֵר (שם ד), תִּתֵּן לְרֹאשְׁךָ לִוְיַת חֵן עֲטֶרֶת תִּפְאֶרֶת תְּמַגְּנֶךָּ. וְאוֹמֵר (שם ט), כִּי בִי יִרְבּוּ יָמֶיךָ וְיוֹסִיפוּ לְךָ שְׁנוֹת חַיִּים. וְאוֹמֵר (שם ג), אֹרֶךְ יָמִים בִּימִינָהּ בִּשְׂמֹאולָהּ עֹשֶׁר וְכָבוֹד, וְאוֹמֵר (שם), כִּי אֹרֶךְ יָמִים וּשְׁנוֹת חַיִּים וְשָׁלוֹם יוֹסִיפוּ לָךְ וְאוֹמֵר (שם), דְּרָכֶיהָ דַרְכֵי נֹעַם וְכָל נְתִיבוֹתֶיהָ שָׁלוֹם:

ח רַבִּי שִׁמְעוֹן בֶּן מְנַסְיָא מִשּׁוּם רַבִּי שִׁמְעוֹן בֶּן יוֹחַאי אוֹמֵר, הַנּוֹי וְהַכֹּחַ וְהָעֹשֶׁר וְהַכָּבוֹד וְהַחָכְמָה וְהַזִּקְנָה וְהַשֵּׂיבָה וְהַבָּנִים, נָאֶה לַצַּדִּיקִים וְנָאֶה לָעוֹלָם, שֶׁנֶּאֱמַר (שם טז), עֲטֶרֶת תִּפְאֶרֶת שֵׂיבָה בְּדֶרֶךְ צְדָקָה תִּמָּצֵא. וְאוֹמֵר (שם יד), עֲטֶרֶת חֲכָמִים עָשְׁרָם.וְאוֹמֵר (שם יז), עֲטֶרֶת זְקֵנִים בְּנֵי בָנִים וְתִפְאֶרֶת בָּנִים אֲבוֹתָם. וְאוֹמֵר (שם כ), תִּפְאֶרֶת בַּחוּרִים כֹּחָם וַהֲדַר זְקֵנִים שֵׂיבָה. וְאוֹמֵר (ישעיה כד), וְחָפְרָה הַלְּבָנָה וּבוֹשָׁה הַחַמָּה, כִּי מָלַךְ יְהוָה צְבָאוֹת בְּהַר צִיּוֹן וּבִירוּשָׁלַיִם וְנֶגֶד זְקֵנָיו כָּבוֹד. רַבִּי שִׁמְעוֹן בֶּן מְנַסְיָא אוֹמֵר, אֵלּוּ שֶׁבַע מִדּוֹת שֶׁמָּנוּ חֲכָמִים לַצַּדִּיקִים, כֻּלָּם נִתְקַיְּמוּ בְּרַבִּי וּבְבָנָיו:

ט אָמַר רַבִּי יוֹסֵי בֶּן קִסְמָא, פַּעַם אַחַת הָיִיתִי מְהַלֵּךְ בַּדֶּרֶךְ וּפָגַע בִּי אָדָם אֶחָד, וְנָתַן לִי שָׁלוֹם, וְהֶחֱזַרְתִּי לוֹ שָׁלוֹם, אָמַר לִי, רַבִּי, מֵאֵיזֶה מָקוֹם אָתָּה, אָמַרְתִּי לוֹ, מֵעִיר גְּדוֹלָה שֶׁל חֲכָמִים וְשֶׁל סוֹפְרִים אָנִי, אָמַר לִי, רַבִּי רְצוֹנְךָ שֶׁתָּדוּר עִמָּנוּ בִּמְקוֹמֵנוּ וַאֲנִי אֶתֵּן לְךָ אֶלֶף אֲלָפִים דִּנְרֵי זָהָב וַאֲבָנִים טוֹבוֹת וּמַרְגָּלִיּוֹת, אָמַרְתִּי לוֹ אִם אַתָּה נוֹתֵן לִי כָל כֶּסֶף וְזָהָב וַאֲבָנִים טוֹבוֹת וּמַרְגָּלִיּוֹת שֶׁבָּעוֹלָם, אֵינִי דָר אֶלָּא בִּמְקוֹם תּוֹרָה, וְכֵן כָּתוּב בְּסֵפֶר תְּהִלִּים עַל יְדֵי דָוִד מֶלֶךְ יִשְׂרָאֵל, טוֹב לִי תוֹרַת פִּיךָ מֵאַלְפֵי זָהָב וָכָסֶף. וְלֹא עוֹד, אֶלָּא שֶׁבִּשְׁעַת פְּטִירָתוֹ שֶׁל אָדָם אֵין מְלַוִּין לוֹ לְאָדָם לֹא כֶסֶף וְלֹא זָהָב וְלֹא אֲבָנִים טוֹבוֹת וּמַרְגָּלִיּוֹת, אֶלָּא תוֹרָה וּמַעֲשִׂים טוֹבִים בִּלְבָד, שֶׁנֶּאֱמַר (משלי ו), בְּהִתְהַלֶּכְךָ תַּנְחֶה אֹתָךְ בְּשָׁכְבְּךָ תִּשְׁמֹר עָלֶיךָ וַהֲקִיצוֹתָ הִיא תְשִׂיחֶךָ, בְּהִתְהַלֶּכְךָ תַּנְחֶה אֹתָךְ, בָּעוֹלָם הַזֶּה. בְּשָׁכְבְּךָ תִּשְׁמֹר עָלֶיךָ, בַּקֶּבֶר. וַהֲקִיצוֹתָ הִיא תְשִׂיחֶךָ לָעוֹלָם הַבָּא. וְאוֹמֵר (חגי ב), לִי הַכֶּסֶף וְלִי הַזָּהָב נְאֻם יְהוָה צְבָאוֹת:

[another verse] says, 'Silver and gold are Mine, says *Adonai Tzevaot*'" [*Hag*. 2:8]

6:10 The Holy One of Blessing marked out five things as divine possessions. They are: the Torah, heaven and earth, Abraham, Israel, and the Temple. How do we know this about the Torah? Because it says, "*Adonai* possessed me in the beginning of the way, before the works of old." [Prov. 8:22] How do we know this about the heaven and earth? Because it says, "The heaven is My throne and the earth is My footstool; what kind of house will you build for Me and what place will be My rest?" [Isa. 66:1] And it says, "*Adonai*, how numerous are Your works! In wisdom You have made them all. The earth is full of Your riches." [Ps. 104:24] How do we know this about Abraham? Because it says, "And God blessed him and said, 'Blessed be Abram of God most high, Possessor of heaven and earth.'" [Gen. 14:19] How do we know this of Israel? Because it says, "Until Your people pass over, *Adonai*, until the people pass over what You have acquired." [Exod. 15:16] And another verse says, "Unto the saints, which are on the earth, and the excellent in whom is My delight." [Ps. 16:3] How do we know this of the Temple? Because it says, "The place, *Adonai*, which You have made for You to dwell in. The sanctuary, *Adonai*, which Your hands have established." [Exod. 15:17] Another verse says. "And God brought them to the border of the sanctuary, to this mountain, which God's right hand had acquired." [Ps. 78:54]

6:11 Whatever the Holy One of Blessing created in the world, God did only for God's own glory, as it says, "Everything that is created for My name, I have created for My glory. I have formed it; indeed, I have made it." [Isa. 43:7] And another verse says, "*Adonai* will reign forever and ever." [Exod. 15:18]

י חֲמִשָּׁה קִנְיָנִים קָנָה לוֹ הַקָּדוֹשׁ בָּרוּךְ הוּא בָּעוֹלָמוֹ, וְאֵלּוּ הֵן, תּוֹרָה קִנְיָן אֶחָד, שָׁמַיִם וָאָרֶץ קִנְיָן אֶחָד, אַבְרָהָם קִנְיָן אֶחָד, יִשְׂרָאֵל קִנְיָן אֶחָד, בֵּית הַמִּקְדָּשׁ קִנְיָן אֶחָד. תּוֹרָה מִנַּיִן, דִּכְתִיב (משלי ח), יְהֹוָה קָנָנִי רֵאשִׁית דַּרְכּוֹ קֶדֶם מִפְעָלָיו מֵאָז. שָׁמַיִם וָאָרֶץ מִנַּיִן, דִּכְתִיב (ישעיה סו), כֹּה אָמַר יְהֹוָה הַשָּׁמַיִם כִּסְאִי וְהָאָרֶץ הֲדֹם רַגְלָי אֵי זֶה בַיִת אֲשֶׁר תִּבְנוּ לִי וְאֵי זֶה מָקוֹם מְנוּחָתִי. וְאוֹמֵר (תהלים קד), מָה רַבּוּ מַעֲשֶׂיךָ יְהֹוָה כֻּלָּם בְּחָכְמָה עָשִׂיתָ מָלְאָה הָאָרֶץ קִנְיָנֶךָ. אַבְרָהָם מִנַּיִן, דִּכְתִיב (בראשית יד), וַיְבָרְכֵהוּ וַיֹּאמַר בָּרוּךְ אַבְרָם לְאֵל עֶלְיוֹן קוֹנֵה שָׁמַיִם וָאָרֶץ. יִשְׂרָאֵל מִנַּיִן, דִּכְתִיב (שמות טו), עַד יַעֲבֹר עַמְּךָ יְהֹוָה עַד יַעֲבֹר עַם זוּ קָנִיתָ, וְאוֹמֵר (תהלים טז), לִקְדוֹשִׁים אֲשֶׁר בָּאָרֶץ הֵמָּה וְאַדִּירֵי כָּל חֶפְצִי בָם. בֵּית הַמִּקְדָּשׁ מִנַּיִן, דִּכְתִיב (שמות טו), מָכוֹן לְשִׁבְתְּךָ פָּעַלְתָּ יְהֹוָה מִקְּדָשׁ אֲדֹנָי כּוֹנְנוּ יָדֶיךָ. וְאוֹמֵר (תהלים עח), וַיְבִיאֵם אֶל גְּבוּל קָדְשׁוֹ הַר זֶה קָנְתָה יְמִינוֹ:

יא כָּל מַה שֶּׁבָּרָא הַקָּדוֹשׁ בָּרוּךְ הוּא בָּעוֹלָמוֹ, לֹא בְרָאוֹ אֶלָּא לִכְבוֹדוֹ, שֶׁנֶּאֱמַר (ישעיה מג), כֹּל הַנִּקְרָא בִשְׁמִי וְלִכְבוֹדִי בְּרָאתִיו יְצַרְתִּיו אַף עֲשִׂיתִיו. וְאוֹמֵר (שמות טו), יְהֹוָה יִמְלֹךְ לְעֹלָם וָעֶד: